# Cowboys, Lawmen, & Outlaws
## The Myth of The American Psyche

By Jerry Bader

MRPwebmedia.com/books

# Cowboys, Lawmen, & Outlaws
## The Myth of The American Psyche

By Jerry Bader
Illustrations by Francisco Ruiz

MRPwebmedia.com/books

**Buffalo Bill Cody**

# Preface
## The Myth of The American Psyche

In the 1950s westerns were the most popular form of television drama. Saturday mornings were filled with black and white images of *Roy Rogers, Gene Autry, The Lone Ranger,* and *The Cisco Kid.* In the evening you had the more adult westerns like *Have Gun, Will Travel, Rawhide,* and *Wanted Dead or Alive.* Sprinkled amongst these shows were programs purporting to be about real historic characters, people like Wyatt Earp, Doc Holliday, Bat Masterson, Annie Oakley, and Wild Bill Hickok.

Although *Gunsmoke's* Marshal Matt Dillon wasn't real, the Long Branch Saloon was. Of course writer John Meston's Matt Dillon was much closer to a real cowboy lawman than what was represented by James Arness. William Conrad's radio version was somehow more real, more colorful, and more dramatic than the whitewashed television version even though the stories were similar. Perhaps it's just a malleable memory but somehow radio always felt more real, more vivid, and more present than television. Television turned everything into pabulum; even fascinating gritty historical characters were turned into cardboard-cutouts designed for the front of cereal boxes featuring the soft mushy historical mess that lay inside. The difference between cowboys, lawmen, and outlaws was merely a cheap metal badge: most often these designations were interchangeable with men easily moving from marshal to villain and back with the deal of a card.

When we think of the Old West, it seems like ancient history, but historically it was yesterday. Many of the characters of the post Civil War Old West lived well into the twentieth century: Bat Masterson died in 1921 and Wyatt Earp didn't pass-on until 1929. Josie Bassett, one of the Wild Bunch girls managed to hang-on until 1963 and she only died then because she got kicked in the head by a horse. History doesn't end with an era, remnants, artifacts, and people overlap. History doesn't stop because technology and style moves on. The future is more likely to look like the movie *Brazil* with its jury-rigged conglomeration of antique flotsam and modern-day technological jetsam, than the bright shiny newness of *Star Trek*. Turning history into fantasy is dangerous; it leads to mistaken notions and bad decisions. Maybe it's time to grow up and see the heroes of the Old West, as they really were, cowboys, lawmen, and outlaws.

The stories that follow are both real and legend. Like much of history, the accounts are blurred, and the memories muddled. Many of the reports have been distorted over time by the telling and retelling as well as the hyperbole of the nineteenth century press and dime novel authors that covered the events.

What is true, at least to this outsider, is that the Old West shaped the American psyche and not necessarily in a good way. Like the Marlboro Man, the myth of the Old West left a cancerous residue that remains to this day. It's a shame these heroes and villains can't just be remembered for who and what they were, cowboys, lawmen, and outlaws.

**Wyatt Earp**

# PART I

# THE INFAMOUS

## Wyatt Earp
### March 19th, 1848 – January 13th, 1929

*"Wyatt Earp was not an angel, but his faults were minor ones, and he never killed a man who did not richly deserve it."*
- George W. Parsons, *Tombstone Times*

I hesitate to start with Wyatt Earp even though he truly is the quintessential iconic symbol of the Old West, strong, tough, handsome, and loyal. He was at various times a gambler, miner, brothel owner, politician, killer, and lawman.

In the case of Wyatt Earp I won't use the term 'Cowboy' to describe him since herding cattle was never on Earp's varied agenda. More significantly in Tombstone in the 1870s and 80s, the term was reserved for a group of cattle rustling ranchers and criminals called the Cochise County

Cowboys, just Cowboys for short. You can't discuss Wyatt Earp without including his brothers, James, Virgil, Morgan, Warren, and of course, his friend John Henry *Doc* Holliday. It's the conflict between the Earp brothers and the Clanton-McLaury Cowboy Gang that cemented the name Wyatt Earp into American history and folklore.

Wyatt Berry Stapp Earp is arguably the most celebrated colorful character of the post, Civil War era. He has been fictionalized and glamorized in movies and television as the hero of the most famous gunfight of the old west, the gunfight at the O. K. Corral. Wyatt was named after his father's commanding officer in the Mexican-American War, Captain Wyatt Berry Stapp, of the 2nd Company Illinois Volunteers. Wyatt was one of the younger Earp children from his father's second marriage. Although he is the most famous Earp, his older brothers James and Virgil and his younger brothers Morgan and Warren were often involved in many of his most well documented incidents along with his pal, the infamous Doc Holliday. What is strikingly clear when reading accounts of the time is that the Earp brothers were loyal to a fault with one another, and that loyalty extended to their close friends and associates, people like Doc Holliday and Bat Masterson.

During the Civil War, Wyatt's father left him and his brothers Morgan and Warren in charge of their Pella Iowa corn farm, while older brothers James, Virgil, and Newton (a half-brother from a previous marriage) joined the Union Army. Wyatt's father spent the war recruiting and training soldiers. Wyatt was only thirteen; too young to join the fighting but that didn't stop him from trying. Each time he ran away to join the army, his father found him and brought him back. During the war James was badly wounded and returned home in 1863. Newton and Virgil survived the fighting intact.

In May of 1864 the Earp family headed west to San Bernardino, California. Along the way, Wyatt assisted his brother Virgil who was a driver for the Banning Stage Coach Line. In 1866 he became a teamster, driving cargo from Wilmington, California to the Utah Territory. In 1868 he was hired to deliver supplies to the Union Pacific Railroad. While working for the railroad he developed his lifelong interests in gambling and boxing, becoming at various times a faro dealer and boxing referee.

In 1868 the family moved to Lamar, Missouri where Wyatt's father, Nicholas, became the local constable. A year later Wyatt joined the family replacing his father as local constable when his father became the Justice of the Peace. In 1870 Wyatt married, but his pregnant wife, Urilla, died of typhoid fever before the end of the year. The death of his wife hit Wyatt hard, leading to a series of legal problems. He failed to hand in all the license fees he was in-charge of collecting, and he was accused of stealing horses. Earp and his accomplices Edward Kennedy and John Shown were arrested but Earp didn't wait around for the trial. He somehow escaped through the jailhouse roof.

Earp headed to Peoria, Illinois where he was arrested several more times for "Keeping and being found in a house of ill-fame," and for operating a floating brothel. On at least one occasion his brother Morgan was also arrested. Wyatt hooked up with a prostitute named Sally Heckell. She began calling herself Sally Earp and referring to herself as Wyatt's wife. Wyatt then moved to Wichita, Kansas in 1874 where Sally and the wife of his brother James were arrested for running a brothel. Wyatt was most likely the house bouncer.

In 1875, newly elected City Marshal Mike Meagher appointed Wyatt a Wichita Deputy City Marshal. Wyatt's stint as Deputy Marshal came to an end when he was fired for breaking the peace as a result of a fist-fight with the former City Marshal Bill Smith who accused Wyatt of stacking the Marshal's office with his brothers. After being fired from his Wichita police job, Wyatt moved to join his brother James who just opened a new brothel in Dodge City.

**Dodge City**
Dodge City was a major hub for the cattle drives that originated in Texas. When the drovers came to town, they

needed to blow-off some steam after the long, dusty, dangerous journey. City Marshal Larry Deger appointed Earp Assistant Marshal. During this period Earp visited the Dakota Territory town of Deadwood that was to become as infamous and storied as Dodge and Tombstone. His time in Deadwood was short-lived as Dodge City Mayor James H. *Dog* Kelley requested he return to resume his policing duties.

In 1877, outlaw, Dave Rudabaugh robbed a Santa Fe Railroad camp. Earp was appointed temporary U. S. Marshal and assigned to track Rudabaugh down. Earp trailed Rudabaugh to the Bee Hive Saloon owned by an old friend, John Shanssey, in Clear Fork, Texas. Shanssey introduced Earp to gambler Doc Holliday, who'd recently played cards with Rudabaugh. Holliday told Earp, Rudabaugh was headed back to Kansas. Earp returned to Dodge empty-handed and was again appointed Assistant Marshal under Charlie Bassett. A short time after, Doc Holliday arrived in town along with his common-law wife, *Big Nose* Kate Elder.

**Virgil Earp**

Morgan Earp

A group of rowdy Texas cowboys headed by Ed Morrison arrived in Dodge firing off their guns causing a considerable disturbance. They proceeded to the Long Branch Saloon where they hassled customers and destroyed property. On hearing the hullabaloo Earp dashed over to the saloon. When he entered he was greeted by a number of guns pointed directly at him. Doc Holliday who just happened to be playing cards in the back of the saloon managed to get the drop on the troublemakers by jamming his revolver into the back of Morrison's head, saving Earp's life. They became close friends for a long time until an unfortunate falling-out years later. During this period in Dodge, Earp also befriended another western legend, Bat Masterson.

**Tombstone**

Wyatt's brother Virgil was town constable in Prescott, Arizona. He wrote Wyatt informing him of the silver prospecting opportunities around Tombstone. Wyatt resigned his position as Assistant Marshal in Dodge and headed for Tombstone with his ex prostitute common-law wife Mattie Blaylock, and his brother James and his wife Bessie. In 1880, after a series of failed attempts at taking advantage of the mining boom, Wyatt hired-on as stagecoach shotgun guard for Wells Fargo. Later that year Morgan and Warren arrived along with Doc Holliday who was flush with forty thousand dollars in gambling winnings. Forty thousand dollars was an enormous amount of money at the time. Holliday was a committed gambler, and questionably an alcohol abuser, but nowhere did I find that Holliday lost that money gambling or making bad investments. It's something to keep in mind in light of future accusations made against him.

The Earps soon came into conflict with a group of outlaw businessmen-ranchers known as 'The Cowboys' led by the McLaury brothers, Tom and Frank, and the Clanton brothers, Ike and Billy. The gang also included Curly Bill Brocius and Frank Stilwell, both of whom played significant roles in future events.

The Cowboys stole six U. S. Army mules from Camp Rucker. U. S. Army Captain Joseph H. Hurst asked for help from U. S. Deputy Marshal Virgil Earp who in turn asked his brothers Wyatt and Morgan, and a Wells Fargo Agent Marshall Williams to form a posse and track down the perpetrators. The posse found the mules on the McLaury Ranch along with the branding iron that was used to re-brand the mules. A deal was struck for the Cowboys to return the mules, which they failed to do. They even laughed at Hurst for expecting them to follow through on their promise. A war of words ensued along with a series of printed flyers exchanging accusations and insults. The Cowboys escalated the situation by threatening to kill the Earp brothers if they ever dared to follow them again.

Later that month Wyatt was appointed Deputy Sheriff for an area that included Tombstone. He turned over his Wells Fargo guard position to his brother Morgan. The Deputy Sheriff's job included duties as county assessor and tax collector. The remuneration for the job was ten percent of the taxes collected; a windfall that could have been as much as forty thousand dollars a year. No doubt the pay was justified by the potentially dangerous nature of the position.

The Earp brothers continued to make enemies when Wyatt pistol-whipped Curly Bill Brocius for accidentally shooting and killing popular town Marshal Fred White. White went to stop a group of Cowboy drunks, including Brocius who were standing in the middle of the street shooting at the moon. Bullets were flying everywhere, and the situation was dangerous. During White's attempt to stop the shooting, Brocius's gun accidentally fired, hitting White in the groin. Wyatt was in the Owens Saloon when he heard the ruckus. By the time he got to the scene, White had been shot.

Earp proceeded to pistol-whip Brocius before arresting him. Marshal White died two days later. Wyatt and Virgil transported Brocius to Tucson for trial or else he might have been lynched for killing the popular marshal. During the trial Wyatt testified evidence showed Brocius's gun went off accidentally, and a gunsmith backed up the claim by testifying the gun was defective. Brocius was cleared and released, however he still held a grudge against all the Earp brothers because of the beating Wyatt gave him, ignoring the fact, Wyatt's testimony helped him beat a murder charge.

Earp's potentially profitable tenure as Deputy Sheriff of Pima County was short-lived when James Johnson, one of the drunken Cowboys involved in the death of Marshal White, fixed a local election by stuffing the ballot boxes with non-eligible voters, including, children, Chinese locals, and enough dogs, burros, and poultry as was needed to get the job done. The results were disputed, but by the time the question of who actually won the election was resolved, the county was redistributed. Cochise County was created out of the eastern part of Pima County.

Republican Earp and his Democratic opponent, Johnny Behan, both intended to run for Sheriff of the newly created Cochise County. The area was mostly Republican but Behan had far more political experience than Earp, so Earp proposed a deal: he would withdraw from the race with the promise from Behan to appoint him Under Sheriff. When the time came, Behan appointed a prominent area Democrat Harry Woods instead of Earp. Behan's excuse was he didn't trust Earp because he warned Ike Clanton about a subpoena he was about to deliver concerning the stolen army mules.

Despite losing the Under Sheriff's job, Wyatt was doing financially well: he and his brothers had made some money from their mining claims. Wyatt also ran a faro concession in the Oriental Saloon, and he acted as the saloon's bouncer. Wyatt brought in his friends Bat Masterson and Luke Short to help with the faro concession.

Earp's reputation was enhanced when he, his brother Virgil, Ben Sippy, and Johnny Behan stood down a mob of angry miners that intended to lynch Michael O'Rouke for killing, Henry Schneider, the popular chief mining engineer for the Tombstone Mining and Milling Company.

Frank Stilwell

**Curly Bill Brocius**

**The Benson Stagecoach Robbery**

The simmering ongoing conflict between the Earp faction and the criminal Cowboy ranchers was the lead-up to what was about to happen next. The following series of events remain unclear as to exactly what happened, but it ended by defining the legend of Wyatt Earp and perhaps came to symbolize the very nature of how America sees itself.

Various reports describe the death of Budd Philpot slightly differently, but in the end the result is the same. On March 15th, 1881, highwaymen murdered Budd Philpot in a failed attempt to rob a Wells Fargo stagecoach carrying a large amount of silver bullion. According to a *Tombstone Times* article on the robbery, when the highwaymen stopped the stagecoach, Bob Paul raised his shotgun and later his revolver and started shooting. He wounded one of the robbers Bill Leonard in the groin. In the ensuing gunfight Philpot was shot and killed. The gunfire spooked the horses, and the stagecoach ran off leaving the robbers empty handed. The robbers chased the stagecoach firing wildly, killing passenger Peter Roerig.

Paul managed to gain control of the reins and make his escape to Benson where he telegraphed back to Tombstone what had happened. Two separate posses were formed, one headed by local Sheriff Johnny Behan, and a more intimidating group headed by Virgil Earp that included Wyatt, Morgan, Bat Masterson, Doc Holliday, and Marshall Williams. The Earp posse eventually caught up with Luther King, one of the robbers who confessed his involvement and implicated Bill Leonard, Harry *The Kid* Head, and Jim Crane as his accomplices. King was turned over to Behan who escorted him back to jail but King immediately escaped, never to be seen or heard from again.

At this point things get even murkier. Doc Holliday left Tombstone earlier that day supposedly on his way to Mexico, or at least, that is what he told people. Somehow he ends up in Charleston asking for Billy Clanton, Ike's younger brother. Supposedly Holliday didn't know Billy, so why would he be looking for him? Holliday reappears in a back alley in Tombstone at around eight-thirty in the evening. Witnesses claim Holliday's horse had been ridden hard as evidenced by the lather. Holliday demanded a drink before even getting off his weary horse. He then joins the Earp posse in the hunt for the robbers.

In the ultimate aftermath of the infamous gunfight on Fremont Street, the McLaurys floated the idea that Doc Holliday was one of the robbers and that he was the triggerman that killed Budd Philpot. The McLaurys claimed Holliday went looking for Billy Clanton in Charleston to kill him because he was a witness to the stagecoach holdup. Personally I think this is nothing more than sour grapes, and a vindictive attempt to get back at the Earp brothers and their friends. Holliday was certainly capable of just about anything but as we remember he came to town with a substantial bankroll, so why would he want to risk robbing a stagecoach? Holliday was a sick man and although he didn't shy away from a gunfight, gambling was about as physical an activity as he was interested in doing.

Although Billy Clanton was known to be in the area the day of the robbery, how likely is it that he just happened to be riding by to witness the robbery; and how could he have recognized Holliday as one of the masked robbers when neither man supposedly knew one another? The McLaurys also floated rumors that the real purpose of the Earp posse was to track down and kill Leonard, Head, and Crane to cover-up Holliday's involvement. The three real robbers were eventually killed attempting to steal cattle from a New Mexico ranch.

**Big Nose Kate Elder: A Woman Scorned**
Holliday and the Earp brothers had enough enemies; they didn't need any more. Holliday's girlfriend, Kate Elder has been described as an educated refined woman in a stable relationship with Holliday, and alternatively, as a bad-tempered drunk in a rocky relationship. The fact is she stayed with Holliday for ten years until he died in 1887. There may have been arguments and Holliday may have thrown Elder out; but more likely, Sheriff Behan, a known Earp enemy, got Elder drunk and had her swear out a

Frank McLaury

Ike Clanton

complaint accusing Holliday of being involved in the holdup. Behan was an old friend with one of the real robbers, Bill Leonard. Holliday was arrested on July 6th, 1881.

Wyatt and his friends were able to put together the five thousand dollars needed to pay Holliday's bail. Marshal Virgil Earp arrested Kate Elder the following day for being drunk and disorderly. After a few days in jail and time to sober up, Elder recanted her complaint and refused to testify. Elder later said she was drunk and didn't know what she signed. The Earps found witnesses to testify that Holliday was seen elsewhere during the time of the murders. The charges against Holliday were dropped.

### The Gunfight At The O. K. Corral

Rumors and speculation were floated by the Clantons that Holliday with the help of the Earp brothers robbed the Benson stagecoach with Billy Clanton just happening to ride by to witness the masked event. Wyatt, his brothers, and Holliday were all well known and recognized in the area. It doesn't make sense that Bob Paul wouldn't have recognized them if they were the robbers, especially when you consider Wyatt had worked for Wells Fargo.

The Clanton and the McLaury brothers hated the Earps and had been threatening retribution for the mule incident for some time. Other Cowboy associates like Curly Bill Brocius hated the Earps, especially Wyatt, for the pistol-whipping he received when he shot and killed Marshal White.

According to Ike Clanton, Wyatt approached him with the promise of a substantial reward if Clanton could setup Leonard and Crane so he could kill them to cover up the robbery that Holliday was involved in. Earp was a lot of things but he wasn't stupid. Why would he admit to such a thing, especially to someone who hated him? Earp's version of what happened makes more sense. He was merely enlisting Clanton's help in tracking down Leonard and Crane since Ike Clanton was a well known go-between for the cattle thieves, ranchers, butchers, and the army.

The reward money was small change compared to what the Clantons earned from their relationship with the thieves. In any case Clanton refused the offer and Leonard and Crane were eventually killed in an attempted rustling in New Mexico.

Ike Clanton and his Cowboy compatriots were going around bragging how they were going to kill the Earps. On Wednesday, October 26th, 1881 everything came to a head. Marshal Virgil Earp learned that the Cowboys were gathering and arming themselves in a vacant lot next to the O. K. Corral near the entrance to Fremont Street. At three o'clock Marshal Virgil Earp, Assistant Marshal Wyatt Earp, Deputy Marshal Morgan Earp, and newly deputized Doc Holliday headed down towards the O. K. Corral to disarm the Cowboys.

When they arrived at the scene near the rear entrance to the O. K. Corral on Fremont they spotted the Cowboys.

They stood only six to ten feet away. Ike Clanton and Billy Claiborne fled while Tom and Frank McLaury, and Billy Clanton stayed to confront the lawmen. The McLaurys and Billy Clanton were killed. Morgan was hit in the shoulder and vertebra; Virgil was shot in the calf; and Holliday received a superficial flesh wound. Wyatt escaped unscathed. In fact in all the various incidents involving gunplay, Wyatt was never wounded.

Ike Clanton filed murder charges against the Earps and Holliday, but a month long hearing proved inconclusive. Testimony for the prosecution proved to be contradictory and confused from so-called witnesses like Sheriff Behan and Ike Clanton who were known to hate the Earps.

**Revenge**

In late December Virgil was severely injured by a shotgun blast to the left arm and shoulder, most likely from Ike Clanton since his hat was found in the alley where the attacker fired. Wyatt requested and was granted appointment as Deputy U. S. Marshal. Clanton was charged but ultimately acquitted when seven people testified he was in Charleston at the time of the shooting.

Morgan was assassinated while playing billiards from another unknown killer that fired through a window from a dark alley. The bullet passed right through Morgan's left side hitting an innocent bystander in the thigh. Another bullet narrowly missed Wyatt. In the prevailing climate Wyatt figured justice would never be served. It was up to him to find and kill those responsible for shooting his brothers.

Wyatt put together a posse that included his brothers James and Warren, Doc Holliday, Sherman McMaster, Jack *Turkey Creek* Johnson, *Hairlip Charlie* Smith, Daniel *Tip* Tipton, and *Texas Jack* Vermillion in order to safeguard the family and track down the suspects. James Earp accompanied Morgan's body back to the family home in Colton, California while the rest of the posse protected Virgil and his wife on their way to Tucson where it was rumored Frank Stilwell was waiting to kill him.

Stilwell's body was found the next day. Warrants were issued for Wyatt and five others. The posse then pursued other members of the Cowboy gang eventually killing *Indian Charlie* Cruz. Wyatt personally shot and killed Curly Bill Brocius and Johnny Barnes, while wounding Milt Hicks in the arm. Sheriff John Behan led a local posse after Wyatt's federal posse but never caught up to them.

Wyatt and his crew then made their way to Albuquerque, in the New Mexico Territory where they met up with Wyatt's old pal U. S. Marshal Bat Masterson. Together they went on to Trinidad, Colorado where Masterson started a faro game in a saloon and later became local Marshal. While in Albuquerque, Wyatt and Holliday had a falling out after Holliday called Wyatt a 'Jew-boy' for staying with a prominent Jewish businessman, Henry N. Jaffa, and for his relationship with Josephine Sarah Marcus, who was also Jewish. Eventually Wyatt made his way to San Francisco where he met up with his girlfriend Josephine Marcus, whom he called Sadie. She remained his common-law wife until Wyatt's death in 1929. Wyatt never divorced his legal wife, Mattie Blaylock, who committed suicide by opium overdose in 1888 in Pinal City, Arizona.

## The Fitzsimmons-Sharkey Fight

Wyatt had a fondness for boxing and over time had refereed over thirty matches. In 1896 he was chosen to referee the most anticipated boxing match in the country, the heavyweight championship between the favored Bob Fitzsimmons and Tom Sharkey. Fitzsimmons dominated the fight but apparently struck Sharkey with a blow below the belt. Earp awarded Sharkey the match for the foul. The crowd was livid and accused Earp of fixing the fight because he bet on Sharkey, but doctors confirmed the low blow after examining him. Fitzsimmons took the matter to court. It was revealed that the promoters had fixed the fight. Earp's previous life as a lawman and gunfighter were used as evidence of his bad character, and his name was smeared in the newspapers throughout the country.

## Life in Los Angeles

In 1910 the Los Angeles Police Department hired sixty-two-year-old Wyatt Earp as a bounty hunter to catch and retrieve criminals that fled to Mexico. Despite his relationship with the police, he never really stayed out of trouble. He was arrested for his involvement in a dispute between the American Trona Company and the California Trona Company over rights to mine potash. In 1911 he was arrested again for an attempted scam involving a fake faro game. Because of his reputation as an authentic western legend, he was sought after by Hollywood producers to act as a non-paid consultant for popular western movies starring people like Tom Mix and William S. Hart.

Wyatt Earp died January 13th, 1929. Josephine, his common-law wife, had him cremated and buried in the family plot at the Hills of Eternity Jewish Cemetery in Colma, California. She died in 1944 and is buried beside him.

**Doc Holliday**

## *Doc* Holliday
## August 14th, 1851 – November 2nd, 1887

*"I found him a loyal friend and good company. He was a dentist whom necessity had made a gambler; a gentleman whom disease had made a vagabond; a philosopher whom life had made a caustic wit; a long, lean blonde fellow nearly dead with consumption and at the same time the most skillful gambler and nerviest, speediest, deadliest man with a six-gun I ever knew"*
– Wyatt Earp as told to Stuart N Lake,
*Wyatt Earp, Frontier Marshal,* 1931

If it wasn't for Wyatt Earp's friendship and the infamous gunfight at the O. K. Corral, it's more than likely that the name and legend of John Henry *Doc* Holliday would have disappeared from history. Holliday is most often misrepresented both in popular culture and sometimes in historical accounts. Even some of the photographs you find have been doctored to show a dark-haired man when in fact Holliday was blond. So who was Doc Holliday and more to the point what brought him to a life of danger, intrigue, and violence? To my mind the Earp quotation that introduces this passage is all you really need to know about who Doc Holliday really was, and why.

Holliday was a well-spoken, educated, Southern gentleman born in Griffin, Georgia; an award-winning dentist; a professional gambler; and a deadly gunfighter. He was tall, thin, blond, and sickly; a slightly built man that occasionally required the aid of a walking stick after being attacked by Henry Kahn in a dispute over a card game. Between his physical build, bad health, and injuries, it's unlikely Holliday was responsible for many of the things attributed to him. He used his reputation as a means to protect himself from those that wished him harm, but when the occasion called for it, he was quite capable of holding his own; not with quick fists, but with his favorite nickel-plated .41 caliber Colt Thunder.

In some accounts Holliday is described as using a shotgun but in reality that only happened once at the gunfight near the O. K. Corral. Carrying guns in Tombstone was contrary to a city ordinance. The McLaurys and the Clantons had been threatening the Earps for some time and were arming themselves in an empty lot near the corral. City Police Chief and U. S. Marshal Virgil Earp formed a posse including his brothers, Wyatt and Morgan, and Doc Holliday in order to confront and disarm the McLaury-Clanton gang. Virgil was legally within his rights to confiscate the weapons of the so-called Cochise Cowboys. He retrieved a messenger shotgun (a sawed-off weapon that could be hidden under a duster) from the Wells Fargo office and handed it to Holliday. The specifics of what happened during the gunfight differ.

It appears Holliday killed Tom McLaury with a shotgun blast from six to ten feet away. In author Stuart Lake's book, *Wyatt Earp, Frontier Marshal,* Earp says Holliday fired the shotgun once; then threw it down in disgust. The kick from the powerful weapon was too much for the slightly built, sickly gambler. According to the account, Holliday then drew his favorite nickel-plated Colt to continue the thirty-second gun battle. At that point things get blurry with everybody but Wyatt either wounded or killed. Holliday was merely grazed by a bullet, but Virgil was shot in the leg and Morgan in the back. Tom and Frank McLaury along with Billy Clanton were killed. Ike Clanton and Billy Claiborne ran off before the shooting started. According to Earp that was the only time Holliday used a shotgun.

Doc was born with a cleft palate that was fixed by his physician uncle, John Stiles Holliday. The birth defect most likely left him with a slight speech impediment. He was named after his Uncle John and his father Henry. His mother Alice died from consumption when Doc was only fifteen years old. His mother's illness most likely was the source of Holliday's tuberculosis, the disease that forced him to abandon his roots; move to the Southwest where the climate was believed to ease his symptoms; and ultimately lead him to into a life of gambling, adventure, and violence. Holliday was loyal to a fault to his friend Wyatt Earp, and despite his reputation, he was not a drunk or prone to excess violence, that is, unless the situation called for it. When all his said and done, it is most likely Holliday only killed one man, Tom McLaury.

John Henry Doc Holliday was not the degenerate drunk stagecoach robber and killer that he has been portrayed. These were accusations and rumors promoted by the McLaury-Clanton Cowboy Gang in concert with other political enemies of the Earps. Holliday was a well-educated, sophisticated professional with a debilitating disease that pushed him into a frontier life of gambling and violence. He was once asked if he ever regretted the things he'd done, or if those things ever bothered his conscience, he replied, *"I coughed that up with my lungs, years ago."* He died from tuberculosis in 1887 at age thirty-six.

**Bat Masterson**

## *Bat* Masterson

### November 26th 1853 – October 25th, 1921

Barclay *Bat* Masterson was born in Quebec, Canada. He was the second oldest of five brothers and two sisters. After brief stints in New York and Illinois, the family found themselves in Wichita, Kansas where Bat remained until his teens, at which time he and two of his brothers left home to become buffalo hunters.

In 1872, Bat and his brother Ed were hired by Raymond Ritter to grade a five-mile stretch of railroad for the Atchison, Topeka & Santa Fe Railroad. Ritter left town without paying the Masterson brothers and their friend Theodore Raymond. Although railroad work was hard, getting paid was harder. It took a year, but on April 15th, 1873 Masterson caught up to Ritter as he arrived in Dodge City carrying a large amount of cash. Masterson boarded the train and confronted Ritter by gunpoint forcing him onto the rear platform in front of a crowd of people where he demanded the three hundred dollars he was owed.

It was this knack for the dramatic that ultimately made Masterson a quintessential western hero. It also illustrates how guns became an integral part of American life, a legacy that remains to this day. The American Constitution maybe the justification for those who want to carry a gun, but the historical, emotional, and psychological rationalization for solving problems with a firearm has deep roots in the pseudo heroes of the Old West.

After Masterson's brief fling as a railroad man he resumed his buffalo hunting activities. The bison were the main source of meat for the Great Plains Native Americans. Millions of these majestic beasts roamed the plains. After the Civil War people started moving out west. An expanded railroad system and military presence was needed to service this western migration. The settlers, soldiers, and railroad men all needed to be fed, and the logical source of food was the millions of bison that roamed the plains. The increasing demand for buffalo hide from back east created an even greater incentive for people like Masterson to become buffalo hunters. There was certainly enough bison to satisfy everyone's real needs, but greed, stupidity, and self-interest turned the buffalo hunt into a mass slaughter leading to the near extinction of the American Buffalo.

This sudden unparalleled slaughter of millions of bison created tension between the combined interests of the military, settlers, and railroads on one side, and the Great Plains Native Americans on the other. Like the Civil War that was at its heart an economic battle fought over human rights, the Indian Wars were an economic battle over the survival of a way of life. In the summer of 1874 Masterson found himself in Adobe Walls, Texas where Comanche leader Quanah Parker led two hundred warriors against the inhabitants of what could loosely be called a town. After five days and many dead warriors Parker retreated. Parker was an interesting character. He was the son of Comanche Chief, Peta Nocona and Cynthia Ann Parker, an English-American who was kidnapped as a child and raised as a Comanche.

In the winter of 1876, in Sweetwater, Texas, Masterson's fought his first and almost his last gunfight. Corporal Melvin A King attacked Masterson, reportedly over a woman, Mollie Brennan, who was killed by a stray bullet from King's gun. Masterson shot and killed King but was himself wounded in the pelvis. A year later Masterson found himself in Dodge City, where he got into a jam when he saved his friend Robert, Bobby Gill, Gilmore from being arrested by the corpulent City Marshal, Larry Deger. Masterson somehow wrapped his arms around the three hundred pound lawman while his friend escaped. No good deed goes unpunished, especially in the Old West. The Marshal's friends grabbed Masterson and held him while Deger beat him senseless.

Masterson was hired as Under-Sheriff of Ford County in 1877. When the current Sheriff, Charles Bassett, was prohibited from running for a third term, Masterson ran and won by a scant three votes. Shortly thereafter being elected, Masterson replaced Larry Deger with his brother Ed as the local City Marshal. Bat and his brother Ed made an effective local policing team by capturing train robbers, Dave Rudabaugh and Ed West, plus two more of their accomplices. The Masterson brothers' crime fighting duo ended when Ed Masterson was shot and killed by Jack Wagner in 1878. Unfortunately for Wagner and his boss Alf Walker, Bat was just across the street. He responded by shooting both men. Wagner died from his wounds the following day, but Walker managed to make his way back to Texas.

Life in the Old West was hard and violent, and you didn't have to be a cowboy or an outlaw to prematurely find your way into a wooden box. In 1878 Dora Hand, a variety actress known as Fannie Keenan was shot and killed by James Kenedy. Masterson formed a posse that included other famous western legends, Wyatt Earp and Bill Tilghman, to track down Kenedy. He was captured the following day after Masterson shot Kenedy in the arm while someone else in the posse shot Kenedy's horse.

At the time the railroads were all competing to dominate the route west. The Santa Fe Railroad and the Denver, Rio

Grande and Western Railway were fighting over the Royal Gorge right-of-way in Colorado. The Santa Fe Railroad enlisted Sheriff Masterson's help to stop their competitor despite the fact Masterson had no official jurisdiction. Masterson recruited a number of men, one of whom might have been Doc Holliday, to help the Santa Fe gain the right of way. Eventually the railroad disagreement was settled, but Masterson's Kansas constituents weren't happy with his out of state activities, so they voted him out of office.

In 1880 Masterson found himself in Dodge City where his brother James was City Marshal. Masterson was summoned by his friend Ben Thompson to help rescue his brother, Billy, who was about to be lynched for shooting the thumb off a fellow named Tucker. Masterson, Ben Thompson, and William F, Cody, better known as Buffalo Bill, got Billy out of town on a midnight train.

In 1882 Masterson was City Marshal of Trinidad, Colorado. He was contacted by his pal, Wyatt Earp, to help stop Doc Holliday from being extradited to Arizona. Masterson went directly to Colorado Governor Frederick W. Pitkin who refused to extradite Holliday. Masterson's involvement in the Holliday incident did not sit well with the voters of Trinidad, but his moonlighting as a faro dealer, was the final straw. He was soundly defeated in the election of 1883.

Masterson's old enemy Larry Deger was now Mayor of Dodge City. Deger had run Masterson's friend Luke Short out of town. Masterson put together a group of gunfighters dubbed 'The Dodge City Peace Commission.' The group included Masterson, Wyatt Earp, Luke Short, Charlie Bassett, and others. The mere presence of the 'Peace Commission' was enough to reinstall Short as a member of the community.

In 1884 while in Dodge, Masterson started his first foray into journalism by publishing a newspaper called *Vox Populi* (Voice of the People), unfortunately despite good reviews, it folded after just one issue. Masterson finally gave up on Dodge and moved to Denver where his reputation as a ladies' man and tough guy followed him. He continued to explore his fondness for gambling and women by dealing faro at Big Ed Chase's Arcade casino. He then purchased the Palace Variety Theater where he became involved with and reportedly married, Indian club swinger and singer Emma Moulton.

Masterson loved boxing so in 1889 he managed to get a job as designated timekeeper at the Sullivan-Kilrain Heavyweight Championship Fight. He was also unofficially in charge of security; it was reported he installed his old friends Luke Short, Johnny Murphy, and twelve other cronies in the crowd in case of trouble. In 1892 Masterson, Luke Short, and fellow Dodge City Peace Commission member, Charlie Bassett attended the Sullivan-Corbett Heavyweight Championship in New Orleans.

In 1895 Masterson moved to New York where he worked for a while as a bodyguard for millionaire George Gould, but by 1897 he was back in Denver managing to get into trouble again. While running for Deputy Sheriff of Arapahoe County he got into a tussle with a Tim Connors ending with another man being shot in the wrist. In 1899 Masterson was the Sports Editor for the Denver newspaper, *George's Weekly*. He also continued his interest in the boxing game by founding the Olympic boxing club after being forced out of the rival Colorado Athletic Association. After selling his Olympic boxing club in 1900, Masterson spent another brief stint in New York, but before long he was back in Denver, but that too, didn't work out well.

There were varying reports as to exactly what happened on his return to Denver; he was either attacked by a woman with an umbrella who objected to him voting in a local election or he was run out of town by the locals for being a drunk.

In 1902 Masterson was back in New York getting into trouble again. He and two other men were arrested on *bunco charges* for attempting to con a Mormon elder out of seventeen thousand dollars. The charges were dropped a few days later, but he was arrested one more time for carrying a concealed weapon. Masterson's Wild West ways were coming into conflict with a changing world; New York wasn't Denver, and the era of the Wild West was over despite the residual psychological impact it had on forming the American psyche.

Masterson's friend Alfred Henry Lewis, a respected investigative journalist and brother of William Eugene Lewis managing editor of the *New York Morning Telegraph*, helped get Masterson a job as a sport's columnist on his brother's newspaper. Lewis introduced Masterson to President Theodore Roosevelt, and they became good friends. Roosevelt appointed Masterson Deputy U. S. Marshal for the Southern District of New York, a post he held until 1909 when he was fired by Roosevelt's successor, William Howard Taft. Masterson continued to cover boxing matches for the *New York Morning Telegraph* until his death from a heart attack at the age of sixty-seven.

**Johnny Ringo**

## Johnny Ringo

### May 3rd, 1850 – July 13th, 1882

Johnny Ringo was associated with the Cochise County Cowboys and was rumored to be involved in the assassination of Morgan Earp. Although his death was ruled a suicide, Wyatt Earp, Doc Holliday, Michael O'Rouke, and Buckskin Frank Leslie were all separately rumored to have killed him.

The Earps and Holliday were sophisticated men; they weren't your average cowboy roughnecks despite their reputations. Johnny Ringo on the other hand appears to be a vile-tempered killer. Ringo was born in Greenfork, Indiana; when he was six his family moved to Liberty, Missouri. His aunt married Cole Younger, a major outlaw figure and member of the James-Younger Gang, a group that included Frank and Jesse James. In 1864 while in Wyoming on the way to California, Ringo's father Martin accidently shot himself in the head with his own shotgun as he stepped off a wagon. Johnny was just fourteen years old.

**The Mason County War (The Hoodoo War)**

In the mid 1870s, Ringo found himself in Mason County, Texas where he became close friends with ex-Texas Ranger Scott Cooley, the adopted son of local rancher Tim Williamson. Like in most disputes, there is a flash point and an underlying cause. American born cattle rustlers Elijah and Pete Backus were taken from their cells and lynched by a mob of German settlers. Shortly thereafter, all hell broke out when Tim Williamson was murdered by a German farmer named Peter Bader.

Underlying this whole dispute was the mistrust and hatred between the American born Texas ranchers and the immigrant German farmers who supported the North during the Civil War. Ringo and his rancher friends went on a rampage against the German settlers. Cooley killed the German ex-Deputy Sheriff, John Worley, the man responsible for protecting Williamson while he was in custody when he was taken and killed by the German settlers, but Cooley didn't just murder him, he scalped Worley and tossed his body down a well.

Ringo and Bill Williams then killed an unarmed James Cheyney in revenge for the ambush murder of Cooley's friend, the popular Moses Baird. Cooley and Ringo then killed Charley Bader, thinking he was Peter. They were arrested but their friends broke them out of jail after which they went their separate ways. Eventually Ringo made his way to Cochise County, where he hooked up with the McLaury-Clanton gang, thereby coming into direct conflict with the Earps and Doc Holliday.

## Suicide or Murder

On July 14th, 1882 John Ringo was found dead from a gunshot to the temple, most probably from the day before based on the state of the body. His remains were found propped up against a large tree with a revolver dangling from his hand. Ringo was buried under the tree. His death was ruled a suicide. Ringo was known to be depressed and rumors floated that he had threatened suicide in the past, but that didn't stop rampant speculation as to what really happened. Here is how the men who found the body described the scene.

"There was a bullet hole in the right temple, the bullet coming out the top of the left side. There is apparently a part of the scalp gone including a small portion of the forehead and part of the hair, this looks as if cut by a knife... He was dressed in light hat, blue shirt, vest, pants and drawers; on his feet were a pair of hose, an undershirt torn up so as to protect his feet. He had evidentially traveled but a short distance in this footgear. His revolver... in his right hand, his rifle rested against the tree close to him. He had on two cartridge belts. The belt for the revolver cartridges... buckled upside on down." The question becomes, what's wrong with this picture?

The men who described the body said the scalp looked like it had been cut with a knife. You would think that these men would know the difference between a bullet wound and a knife wound. So why would Ringo try to scalp himself? That just doesn't make sense. The fact that his feet were wrapped in a torn undershirt sounds weird but some have explained it away as common practice at the time. Cowboys would tie their boots to their saddle at night to avoid waking up the next day to find scorpions in them. When they found Ringo's horse a few days later, his boots were tied to his saddle, but if Ringo was going to commit suicide, why would he remove his boots and wrap his feet?

The men described Ringo *"dressed in a light hat"* which seems to mean he was wearing the hat when they found him. If the hat was beside him on the ground wouldn't witnesses have said that? They obviously must have removed the hat in order to describe the condition of his head, but somehow no mention is made of a bullet hole in the hat. This seems impossible since the bullet exited his head lodged in the tree. It would seem reasonable to assume someone put the hat on his head after he was killed. And then there's the upside-down cartridge belt. It certainly appears that someone else hastily put the belt on the dead body without realizing, or worrying, that it was upside-down.

Testimony also stated that Ringo's gun only contained five cartridges. Reports written many years later stated that a sixth empty cartridge was found in the gun, but that appears to be the untrustworthy recollection of an old-timer recalling events from long ago. It was common practice to only have five cartridges in a gun leaving one chamber empty to avoid accidentally shooting yourself, or someone else. This was what happened when Curly Bill Brocius shot and killed Marshal Fred White and remember, Ringo's father inadvertently shot and killed himself when his shotgun misfired. It would seem likely that Ringo would have learned his lesson about handling guns.

From here on the story gets even more muddled, melding witness testimony, blurry recollections, and conspiracy theories based on various events and conflicts that were happening at the time.

### Did Frank *Buckskin* Leslie Kill Ringo?

While serving time in a Yuma prison for killing his wife, Leslie reportedly told a guard he was the one that killed Johnny Ringo in order to curry favor with Wyatt Earp.

Earp suspected that Ringo was involved in the murder of his brother Morgan. There is also an unsubstantiated story that when Leslie shot and killed Billy Claiborne, one of the McLaury-Clanton gang, his dying words were, "*Frank Leslie killed John Ringo. I saw him do it.*" Newspaper reports at the time only stated that Leslie killed Claiborne over a political disagreement, but exactly what does that mean? Tombstone politics were based on who was going to control Cochise County, the Earps or the McLaury-Clanton gang.

**Did Wyatt Earp Kill Ringo?**
According to Frank Lockwood's book *Pioneer Days in Arizona* (1932), Earp told him he killed John Ringo and Curly Bill Brocius when the Earps went after Morgan's killers and whoever shot Virgil. Since Earp died in 1929, there was no way to verify the claim, however Earp did deny killing Ringo when interviewed in Denver in 1896. Since Brocius and Ringo were killed three months apart, many believe it's unlikely that Earp killed both men.

## Did Doc Holliday Kill Ringo?

Holliday was part of the Wyatt Earp posse that sought revenge for the ambush of Virgil and Morgan Earp. Holliday was close friends with Earp and consistently backed his friend in any dispute. It's not unreasonable to believe Holliday shot Ringo for his friend Wyatt, however, there is evidence that Holliday was in Pueblo County at the time. Holliday supposedly appeared in the Pueblo County District Court based on court documents that state Holliday appeared in court, *"in his own proper person as well as his attorney."* The evidence seems to clear Holliday, but not so fast; others claim the legalese is mere court boilerplate and perhaps only Holliday's lawyer actually appeared.

So did Johnny Ringo wrap his feet in a torn undershirt, put his cartridge belt on upside-down, shoot himself in the head, and then put his hat on? Or did Frank Leslie, Wyatt Earp, or maybe Doc Holliday kill him? Nobody knows for sure. I leave that for you to decide.

**Doc Scurlock**

## Josiah Gordon *Doc* Scurlock
## January 11th, 1849 – July 25th, 1929

Doc Holliday wasn't the only southern medical man that turned out to be a gunfighter. Doc Scurlock may not be as famous as Holliday but he was just as deadly, and probably responsible for more dead bodies than Holliday. Unlike Holliday who was an expert dentist that continually practiced his trade when it didn't interfere with his gambling and gun fighting duties, there appears to be only brief references to Scurlock practicing medicine. Like Holliday, Scurlock wasn't just some common thug, he was an educated southern gentleman who in addition to his vigilante career was at times a physician, teacher, farmer, candy store owner, poet, and author. Not the resume of your average murdering cowboy bad guy.

After his medical studies he found himself in Mexico where he got into an argument with an opponent over a card game. Both men drew their guns but the other man fired first hitting Scurlock in the mouth knocking out his front teeth. The bullet exited the back of his neck without causing any more significant damage. Despite Scurlock's injuries, he had the presence of mind to fire back killing his attacker.

On his return to the States he joined up with cattle baron, John Chisum, to help protect his herd from rustlers and Indian attacks. While working for Chisum he had several run-ins with the Indians. Scurlock narrowly escaped being killed when he and his riding partner Jack Holt were attacked, unfortunately Holt wasn't as lucky. His partially dismembered body was found several days later with its right arm removed at the elbow. A couple of years later, Scurlock and his new partner Newt Higgins were attacked, and Higgins was killed. Scurlock figured his luck was running out, so he told Chisum he was quitting. Chisum refused to pay him so Scurlock stole three horses, two saddles, and a rifle and headed for Arizona. Chisum sent a posse of men after him but when they caught up to Scurlock he justified his behavior by explaining Chisum wouldn't pay him his back pay. The men agreed with Scurlock's actions and let him go.

In Arizona he became friends with Charlie Bowdre and together the two men opened a cheese factory of all things. Henry McCarty, also known as William H. Bonney, and more famously Billy the Kid, was one of their first employees. After closing the factory the two friends bought a ranch on credit from Lawrence G. Murphy in Lincoln County, New Mexico. Bowdre and Scurlock married the Herrera sisters becoming brothers-in-law as well as best friends.

Scurlock and Bowdre were involved in numerous posses tracking down and lynching a number of horse and cattle thieves. Murphy and his partner James Dolan continually overcharged the small ranchers and farmers for their goods. To combat the Murphy & Dolan Mercantile and Banking Company's hold on trade, John Tunstall and lawyer, Alexander McSween opened a rival business backed by powerful rancher John Chisum.

## The Lincoln County War

Dolan hired groups of gunfighters including the Seven Rivers Warriors, the Jesse Evans Gang, and the John Kinney Gang to harass and steal Tunstall-McSween cattle. In response Tunstall hired his own group of gunmen including Scurlock, Bowdre, Dick Brewer, and Billy the Kid to combat the Murphy-Dolan group.

Things got worse when Tunstall, himself, was killed on orders from Dolan. The local sheriff was too corrupt to do anything about the murder, so Alex McSween formed the Lincoln County Regulators. He had them legally deputized in order to track down the murderers and bring them to justice. Scurlock was one of the original members. The war continued with numerous killings on both sides. Scurlock eventually became the leader after two of his predecessors were killed. Among the Regulator victims were the sheriff and his deputy, both Dolan supporters. McSween loyalist John Copeland was appointed sheriff and Scurlock his deputy. Dolan loyalist George Peppin eventually replaced Copeland as sheriff.

After a failed attempt to make peace with Dolan; after witnessing Dolan and his men murder Sue McSween's lawyer; and after Governor Lew Wallace failed to grant a promised pardon to Billy the Kid for testifying against the murders, Scurlock, Billy the Kid, Charlie Bowdre, and other former Regulators formed a new gang called The Rustlers. The gang stole one hundred and eighteen head of cattle from Chisum, so the law came after them hard. With the heat on Scurlock, he left Lincoln County for Tascosa, Texas. Scurlock kept a low profile in Texas moving around doing various jobs until in 1919 he settled down in Eastland County and became a respected member of the community as the owner of a candy store. He died in 1929.

**Tom Horn**

## Tom Horn, Jr.

### November 21st, 1860 – November 20th, 1903

*"Killing men is my specialty. I look at it as a business proposition, and I think I have a corner on the market."* - Tom Horn

Much of history, including the era of the Old West, has been corrupted by sanitized retellings on television and in the movies, especially in the early days of TV. All the characters have been divided into either black hats or white hats, and all their stories have been refashioned into good versus evil morality plays. The Old West was far more complex; far more nuanced; and far grayer than it was black or white. Failure to learn from history, real history, is a grave national mistake. To understand who you are, rather than who you think you are, requires an understanding of where you came from, not a fantasized blurry make-believe version suitable for a G-rated audience.

The men and even some of the women in this book were killers, thieves, and drunks, but many of these same men, as we have already seen, were also lawmen, heroes, and political strategists that helped open the west to eventual structured governance. Tom Horn as much as anyone else represents this dichotomy; he was an effective scout and interpreter for the military; a brave hero in battle, a successful and deadly detective, and a dangerous hired killer that was hanged for a murder he may not have committed.

Horn was born in 1860 in Scotland County, Missouri to authoritarian, strict, violent, and religious parents, Thomas S. Horn, Sr. and Mary Ann Maricha. Tom's childhood was not a happy one; he suffered at the hands of an abusive father and the neighborhood bullies. At sixteen he headed west becoming a civilian scout and interpreter for the U. S. Cavalry. Horn distinguished himself during the Apache Wars both as a scout, tracking down Geronimo's major stronghold, and as a hero in the Battle of Big Dry Wash. For his bravery he was named Chief of

Scouts for Captain Emmet Crawford, commander of Fort Bowie. In 1886, Horn acted as interpreter for First Lieutenant Charles Bare Gatewood at the historic final surrender of Geronimo.

With his earnings from the military Horn started a ranch with a hundred head of cattle and twenty-six horses in Aravaipa Canyon, Arizona. Unfortunately rustlers raided his ranch and stole his entire stock forcing him into bankruptcy. The experience instilled in Horn a life long hatred of thieves and rustlers. The rest of his life was motivated by a search for vengeance as a vigilante and range detective charged with protecting ranchers from thieves. If he suspected someone of stealing, they would be warned; if they didn't heed his warning, they would turn up dead. According to reports, Horn's presence was often enough to send potential thieves packing.

**The Pleasant Valley War**

Horn worked for Robert Bowen during the Pleasant Valley War, also referred to as the Tonto Basin Feud and the

Tewksbury-Graham Feud between cattle and sheep ranchers. The feud lasted ten years from 1882 to 1892 with an estimated thirty-five to fifty casualties. The dispute was so vicious and disruptive that it almost wiped out all the male members of two families and delayed statehood for Arizona by ten years. In Horn's autobiography that he wrote while in jail waiting to be hanged, he claims that during this time he was a Deputy Sheriff for three well-known Arizona lawman, William Owen *Bucky* O'Neill, Commodore Perry Owens, and Glen Reynolds. He also claims he acted as a mediator in the dispute. However his form of mediation appears to have resulted in the disappearance of Mart Blevins and the lynching of three suspected rustlers with the help of Glen Reynolds.

His involvement in arguably the bloodiest range war in the Old West, his known tracking ability, his coolness under fire, and his willingness literally to execute a final result drew the attention of the Pinkerton Detective Agency. In late 1889 or early 1890 Horn was hired by Pinkerton to work out of the Denver office handling cases in Colorado, Wyoming, and other western states.

## The Johnson County War

During the Johnson County War while still working for Pinkerton, Horn signed on to work for the Wyoming Stock Growers Association. During this time he is rumored to have killed numerous men including Nate Champion, Nick Ray, John A. Tisdale, and Orley *Ranger* Jones. By 1892 it appears Horn's high profile was making the Pinkerton bosses nervous, so he was forced to resign. For the next few years Horn acted as a hired killer, euphemistically referred to as a range detective, hired to protect the stock of various ranchers, and rid the area of the cattle and horse thieves. In his capacity as a so-called range detective he was both bloody and effective, leaving a long trail of dead bodies.

## The Colorado Range War

During the Colorado Range War, Horn was employed by the Swan Land and Cattle Company to work undercover as Tom Hicks. He was hired to investigate the Browns Park Cattle Association leader Matt Rash who was suspected of cattle rustling. In fact both sides in this dispute were guilty of stealing. Horn waited until he had enough evidence against Rash to prove he was guilty. He posted a note on Rash's cabin door warning him to leave in sixty days. When Rash ignored the warning, Horn was given the go-ahead to kill him, which he did one morning while Rash was eating breakfast. Rash attempted to write the killer's name in blood but he failed to leave any legible evidence. Horn's main accuser was Ann Bassett a neighboring rancher who was engaged to Rash.

Ann and Josie Bassett were intimate friends and associates of the Wild Bunch, which is most likely the reason Horn left them alone. Instead, he zeroed in on Rash and Isom Dart. Dart worked for Rash and was pretty much known to be the former cattle thief Ned Huddleston, the only surviving member of the Tip Gault Gang. Rumors were spread that Dart killed Rash, but it seems these rumors were spread to remove suspicion from Horn. Dart was the pasty. In order to tie-up loose ends, Horn murdered Dart.

## The Will Nickell Murder

In 1901 after serving as an outfitter in the United States Army during the Spanish American War, Horn returned to Iron Mountain in Wyoming to visit Jim and Dora Miller. Miller was having a dispute with his neighbor Kels Nickell over Nickell's introduction of sheep into the area. Miller accused Nickell of allowing his sheep to graze on his land. The feud extended to the children who often replicated their parents' dispute at school. Fourteen-year-old Willie Nickell was found dead on July 18th, 1901 near the Nickell's homestead gate. Other violent incidents continued during the time of the investigation into Willie's death culminating in the wounding of Kels Nickell, and the slaughter of sixty-to-eighty of his sheep. Two of Nickell's children spotted two men riding away from the scene on what appeared to be recognizable Miller horses. Jim Miller and two of his sons were arrested for wounding Kels Nickell.

Months later Deputy Marshall Joe Lefors ostensibly talked to Horn about employment while he was drunk. Lefors claimed Horn bragged to him about killing Willie with his rifle from three hundred yards away, bragging that it was the *"best shot that (he) ever made and the dirtiest trick that (he) ever done."* This claim doesn't seem to make sense. Why would Horn confess to a murder? Why would he kill a fourteen-year-old kid without warning when it was known that he almost always warned his victims? The story doesn't add up. In any case Horn was arrested the next day. The trial judge, Richard H. Scott, was up for re-election, prompting a quick guilty verdict, and what better solution than to convict an outsider.

Horn was supported by friend and cattle rancher John C. Coble as well as members of the Wyoming Stock Growers Association. A large expensive legal team was put in place to defend him, but rumor had it that they put up only a minimal defense, as Horn knew far too much about the Association's illegal activities. The evidence presented against Horn was circumstantial, and there were no collaborating witnesses to the drunken so-called confession. Other witnesses claimed Horn was seen twenty miles away only an hour after the murder. Despite logic and the discrepancies Horn was found guilty and sentenced to death by hanging. Horn's lawyers applied for a new trial but were denied despite appeals to the Governor from an ex local schoolteacher who blamed Jim Miller for the murder. The Wyoming Supreme Court denied Horn a new trial. He was hanged on November 20th, 1903, one day before his forty-third birthday.

The verdict in the case is disputed with adherents on both sides. Those that knew Horn the best did not believe he did it and there was no physical evidence to link him to the murder. In addition, witnesses recall him being far from the sight of the crime when the murder took place. It appears that Horn was convicted as a convenient scapegoat on reputation rather than on the facts of the case.

Wild Bill Hickok

## James Butler *Wild Bill* Hickok
### May 27th, 1837 – August 2nd, 1876

*"I don't like to talk about that McCanles affair. It gives me a queer shiver whenever I think of it, and sometimes I dream about it and wake up in a cold sweat."*
– James Butler 'Wild Bill' Hickok

James Butler Hickok was born in Homer, Illinois (present-day Troy Grove) to William Alonzo and Polly Hickok. His father was a farmer and an abolitionist that used his home as a way station on the Underground Railroad. Young James Butler was the fourth of six Hickok children and was known to be an excellent marksman. Although he is most often depicted with dark hair, he was usually described as a redhead. This appears to be common at the time as we've already learned from the retouched photographs of Doc Holliday depicting him with dark hair when in fact he was blond.

In 1855 Hickok, who had a reputation as a ruffian, got into a fight with Charles Hudson that ended with both men falling into a canal thinking each had killed the other. Hickok fled to the Kansas Territory where he joined General Jim Lane's anti-slave guerrilla free-state army, known as the Jayhawkers. During this period he met a very young William Cody who was acting as a scout for the U. S. Army involved in the Utah Campaign also referred to as the Mormon Rebellion.

Before Hickok's legendary reputation and famous *Wild Bill* nickname became common knowledge, he was mockingly called *Duck Bill* due to his large nose and protruding upper lip. He was also called *Shanghai Bill* due to the fact he was tall and thin. The Wild Bill designation became legend after Hickok killed ex-sheriff, rancher, bully, and alleged outlaw gang leader David McCanles and several of his men. Whether McCanles was in fact a criminal is in dispute by some historians although he does nicely fit the mold of similar rancher-outlaw criminals like the Clantons and the McLaurys.

Some chalk the incident up to a dispute over a woman that was exacerbated by the insults McCanles hurled at Hickok over his big nose and Duck Bill nickname, but there is reason to believe that McCanles' criminal activity also contributed to the hostility.

**The Rock Creek Incident**
In 1860 Hickok signed on as a freight driver for Russell, Waddell & Majors, the parent company of the Pony Express. While driving freight from Independence, Missouri to Santa Fe, New Mexico Hickok encountered a cinnamon bear and her cubs blocking their way. According to Hickok he confronted the bear on foot, shooting it in the head and paw. Despite being wounded, the bear still managed to crush Hickok's chest, shoulder, and arm before Hickok was able to kill it by slashing its throat with his knife. Hickok spent four months in bed recovering after which he was sent to Rock Creek Station in the Nebraska Territory in what was expected to be a rehabilitation stint. The Rock Creek station, managed by Horace Wellman, was built on land purchased from David McCandles.

The freight company fell behind its payments to McCanles for the land. McCanles, his son Monroe (maybe William), his cousin James Woods, and an employee James Gordon arrived at the station on July 12th, 1861 demanding to see Wellman in order to settle the outstanding debt. At this point the incident gets blurry. McCanles entered the station and confronted Wellman and his wife regarding payment. An argument must have got out of hand because Hickok who was hiding behind a curtain shoots and kills the supposedly unarmed McCanles.

Hearing the gunshots, McCanles's son rushes into the station to help his father. The unarmed Woods and Gordon attempt to escape. Hickok goes after Woods and Gordon wounding both men while McCanles's son escapes. Gordon was killed with a shotgun blast from station employee Doc Brink. Woods was killed by Wellman or his wife, who reportedly hacked him to death with a gardening hoe.

The incident firmly established Hickok's reputation as a gunman, making it easy for him to demand the Wild Bill designation, rather than the derogatory Duck Bill. In order to complete the gunslinger look Hickok grew his distinguishing mustache in order to hide his protruding upper lip. His reputation was further enhanced years later when an article in *Harper's Monthly* described Wild Bill Hickok as the hero that single-handedly saved the Rock Creek stagecoach and mail station by killing members of the dangerous and violent McCanles Gang.

**The Civil War**

In 1861 Hickok joined the Union Army as a teamster working his way up to wagon master. In 1862 he was mysteriously discharged. He then joined Senator and Union General, James Henry Lane's Kansas Brigade where he is rumored to have acted as a Union spy in Confederate territory. In 1863 he was a military policeman working for the provost marshal of southwest Missouri. As a military policeman he checked liquor licenses, watched for drunken uniformed soldiers, and collected funds owed to the Union Army. After the war he went to Springfield where he began gambling.

## The Gunfights

While in Springfield Hickok continued gambling, losing money to Davis Tutt. Unable to collect what he was owed, Tutt stole Hickok's watch. The dispute was intensified by the fact both men were fond of the same woman. The disagreement finally culminated in what is considered the first prototypical quick draw gunfight. On July 21st, 1865 the two men faced off in the middle of the Springfield town square.

Hickok and Tutt were described as standing sideways about seventy-five yards apart when they drew their guns and fired. Tutt's shot missed but Hickok's didn't. Tutt was supposedly heard crying out "Boys, I'm killed" before collapsing and dying from the bullet to his chest.
Hickok was arrested for manslaughter and tried. The judge gave conflicting instructions to the jury: on the one hand he instructed the jury the only verdict they could

deliver was guilty; on the other hand he told them they could acquit if they applied the unwritten fair fight law. The jury chose to acquit. Later in 1865 Hickok lost the election for City Marshal of Springfield but was recommended for the job of Deputy U. S. Marshal at Fort Riley, Kansas.

In 1867 in Jefferson County, Nebraska Hickok had a run-in with someone who pushed him, causing him to drop his drink. After Hickok hit the man, four of his friends drew their guns, but Hickok convinced them to take their dispute out to the street. The bartender counted down as Hickok faced the four men. He killed three of them and wounded the fourth. He was hit in the shoulder.

Hickok moved on to Hays City, Kansas and in 1868 became the Deputy U. S. Marshal. A year later he was elected City Marshal and Sheriff of Ellis County, Kansas. Hickok quickly established himself as the law in town by killing two men in his first month in office. A drunken Bill Mulvey started shooting up the town. When he was warned to cut it out or Hickok would make him, he threatened to kill Hickok. He finally faced Hickok in the street while on his horse. He leveled his rifle at Hickok who then waved at some bystanders to not shoot him in the back. When Mulvey turned to look, Hickok shot him in the head killing him.

When Hickok and his deputy went to quell a disturbance at a local saloon, they found Samuel Strawhun was causing a drunken ruckus. On seeing Hickok, Strawhun made some disparaging remarks resulting in Hickok shooting him in the head. In a separate incident, two soldiers attacked Hickok in a saloon. One of the men pinned Hickok to the floor while the other put his gun to Hickok's ear and pulled the trigger. The gun misfired. Hickok shot the man pinning him in the knee. He then shot and killed the soldier whose gun misfired. When the next election rolled around Hickok wasn't reelected.

In 1871 Hickok became Marshal in Abilene, Kansas replacing murdered Marshal Tom *Bear River* Smith. Known gunfighter John Wesley Hardin using the alias Wesley Clemmons arrived in town with a group of cowboys driving cattle. Hardin is said to have killed twenty-seven men. Hickok and Hardin became friends although Hickok later said he didn't know Clemmons was the wanted criminal John Wesley Hardin. In August of that same year Hickok tried to arrest Hardin for killing Charles Couger for snoring too loudly. Hardin left the state before Hickok could arrest him.

## The Bulls Head Tavern Incident

People in the Old West were killed for all kinds of reasons. If you could get killed by one of the West's most notorious gunfighters for snoring too loudly, anything is possible. Phil Coe and his gambler partner Ben Thompson owned a saloon called *The Bull's Head Tavern*. The problem started when the saloon owners painted a logo on the side of the saloon. The townsfolk objected to the logo and wanted it removed as they deemed it objectionable. You may ask, why would a logo of a bull's head be objectionable and of course, the answer is, it isn't. Instead of just a bull's head,

Coe and Thompson thought it would be clever to paint a logo of a bull complete with an erect penis. Hickok went to Coe requesting that he remove the logo but Coe refused, so Hickok removed it for him.

Coe was so angry he approached Hardin to kill Hickok to which Hardin replied, "If Bill needs killing why don't you do it yourself?" As usual what happened next is up for debate. What is known is a group of drunken cowboys started a brawl in the middle of the street. The disturbance was most likely orchestrated by Coe in order to attract Hickok's attention. Coe's plan was to kill Hickok in the confusion. As Hickok tried to face down the drunken cowboys, Coe fired two shots claiming he was firing at a stray dog.

Hickok ordered Coe arrested for firing a gun within city limits. Coe objected and took aim at Hickok, but Hickok fired first killing Coe. During the confusion Hickok spotted someone run at him; he turned quickly and fired two shots killing whoever it was. Unfortunately the person

Hickok spotted coming at him was his own Deputy Marshal Mike Williams, who was coming to help. Mayor Theo Little claimed Williams ran in front of Hickok just as he was attempting to shoot Coe. According to Mayor Little, Hickok then fired killing Coe. In either case, Hickok regretted the William's shooting for the rest of his life. Two months after the incident, Hickok was removed as marshal.

Hickok appeared along with Buffalo Bill Cody and Texas Jack Omohundro in a play, *Scouts of the Plains*. Hickok eventually tired of acting and left the show. Around this time he was diagnosed with glaucoma; his skills and health were starting to fail. In 1876 Hickok married Agnes Thatcher Lake, a circus owner in Cheyenne, Wyoming Territory. Although there are no records to prove it, other than by her own account, Martha Jane Cannary (Calamity Jane) claimed she was married to Hickok and divorced him so he could marry Lake. Shortly after marrying Lake, Hickok hooked up with Charlie Utter; the two men headed to South Dakota to prospect for gold.

## Deadwood

On his arrival in Deadwood, Dakota Territory, Hickok decided he preferred gambling to prospecting. He spent most of his time playing poker at the Nuttal & Mann Saloon. On the night before his murder, Jack McCall joined Hickok's poker game. McCall lost heavily and resented Hickok's efforts to get him to quit. McCall refused and continued until he lost everything. Hickok offered McCall money for breakfast and although he accepted the cash, he resents the fact Hickok offered. The following evening Hickok joins a poker game with Charles Rich and riverboat captain William Massie. The only seat available at the table is the one placing Hickok with his back to the door. Hickok always played facing the door. He asked Rich to switch seats two times, but Rich refused. Hickok decides to play anyway. McCall still fuming from his poker losses and the perceived insults from the night before comes up behind Hickok and shoots him in the back of his head with an eighteen-inch Sharps revolver. The bullet passes through Hickok's cheek, entering Massie's left wrist. James Butler *Wild Bill* Hickok is dead.

Deadwood was in Indian Territory so there was no official law or government authority. The local informal Deadwood *miners jury* found McCall not guilty based on the unsupported claim that McCall killed Hickok as revenge for Hickok killing his brother in Abilene. Although a Lew McCall was killed in Abilene by an unnamed lawman, no one knows if this Lew McCall was actually related to Jack McCall, or if the lawman in question was Hickok. McCall was rearrested in Yankton, Dakota. The original trial had no legal or official standing. McCall was tried, convicted, and hanged on March 1st, 1877.
There is no evidence that Hickok was holding, the so-called *Dead Man's Hand*, a pair of black aces and a pair of black eights when he was shot.

John Wesley Hardin

## John Wesley Hardin
## May 26th, 1853 – August 19th, 1895

*"They say I killed six or seven men for snoring. Well, it ain't true. I only killed one man for snoring."* – John Wesley Hardin

Like most of the men and women of the post Civil War era, John Wesley Hardin was a dichotomy; although he was defined by the twenty-seven men he killed, he was also a well-spoken southern gentleman, a lawyer brought up by a charitable mother and minister-teacher father. He was named after John Wesley, founder of the Protestant Methodist denomination. Hardin was fond of saying *"he never killed anyone that didn't need killing,"* a bold claim for someone with at least twenty-seven notches on his belt. Despite the trail of dead bodies he left in his wake he did have some sort of moral compass or at least a delusional self-justification. To his credit he refused to kill Bill Hickok.

When Hardin was only nine-years-old he tried to run away and join the Confederate Army. Trouble started when in

1867 while he was still a student in his father's school; he stabbed a classmate, Charles Sloter, who accused him of writing defamatory graffiti on the schoolhouse wall about a female student. Hardin claimed it was Sloter who was responsible. Sloter responded by attacking Hardin with a knife but Hardin responded by almost killing Sloter with his own knife.

A year later when Hardin was fifteen, he challenged his uncle's former slave Maje to a wrestling match. He won the fight but according to Hardin, Maje attacked him the following day; Hardin responded by pulling his revolver and shooting him five times. Maje died three days later. Hardin's father sent him into hiding, figuring there was no way he would get a fair trial. Union soldiers occupied the state and a third of the police force were former slaves. Soldiers were sent to apprehend Hardin but his brother warned him they were coming. When the soldiers finally caught-up to him, he greeted them with a double-barreled shotgun. He killed four of them but was wounded in the arm.

Hardin went on the run with a fellow outlaw Frank Polk. Polk was eventually captured but Hardin escaped, and for a while taught school in Pisgah, Texas. After several more killings Hardin ended up in Towash Hill County where he got into a card game with Benjamin Bradley. Hardin was winning almost every hand, angering Bradley who threatened, *"to cut out his liver"* if he won another hand, but Hardin kept on winning. Bradley responded by drawing his gun and a knife but Hardin was unarmed, so Bradley backed off and Hardin left. Later that night Bradley came looking for Hardin, but this time Hardin was prepared. In front of numerous witnesses Bradley fired at Hardin but missed. Hardin responded by firing both his pistols, hitting Bradley with one bullet in the head and another in the chest. Hardin had his holsters sewn to his vest so that the gun butts faced across his body; he drew by crossing his hands across his chest to access the revolver on the opposite side. This was a move Hardin practiced until he had perfected it, making him the most deadly gunfighter in the Old West.

There is some evidence to back up Hardin's claim that he only shot people who intended to harm him. As stated earlier he had no argument with Bill Hickok so he had no reason to shoot him, and when a posse of fifteen men were sent after him as a result of the Bradley shootout, he ended up capturing two of the men, disarmed them, and sent them on their way. That said, Hardin defined people who intended to harm him rather broadly. He killed a number of men for relatively trivial matters. While walking a saloon girl home, Hardin was confronted by the girl's pimp who demanded money. Hardin threw the money on the ground and when the pimp bent over to pick it up, Hardin shot him. He killed another man over an argument at a circus. Like I said, his definition of harm was broadly interpreted.

In January 1871, seventeen-year-old Hardin was arrested in Marshall, Texas for murdering Waco City Marshal, John Hoffman. Hardin denied the charges. While in jail, Hardin bought a gun from a fellow prisoner. Two state policemen were assigned to deliver Hardin to Waco for trial. On the way, Hardin claimed he was left alone with one of the men, while the other man went to purchase feed for the horses. While alone the man left to guard Hardin, started to taunt and beat him. Hardin drew his gun and killed the guard. He escaped on the policeman's horse.

When he was arrested again; he somehow managed to kill all three of his captors with their own guns. Hardin then went south to Gonzales, Texas where he hid out with his cousins. They suggested he join a cattle drive to Kansas in order to make some money and get out of the state. Hardin's violent streak continued with him pistol-whipping a Mexican and shooting two others over a game of three-card Monte.

While on the cattle drive Hardin claims to have shot a number of Mexican *vaqueros* along with a number of Indians that interfered with their progress. Although these claims seem to have been exaggerated, the fact is, Hardin was responsible for a number of killings along the way. The trouble didn't stop when Hardin arrived in Abilene where he got into another shooting, forcing him to escape to the Cottonwood Trail where he killed the Mexican responsible for killing William Cohron, his trail boss.

**The Snoring Man Incident**

Hardin was in Abilene with his cousin Gip Clements and a friend Charles Couger. The three were staying in the American Hotel with Clements and Hardin sharing one room and Couger in the room next door. The men spent the evening drinking so by the time they went to bed they were thoroughly drunk. During the night Couger's drunken snoring woke Hardin. He shouted for him to rollover and shut up but Couger was in no condition to respond. Frustrated and still drunk himself, Hardin fired several gunshots into the wall of Couger's room with the intent of waking him up, but instead, one of the bullets hit Couger in the head killing him instantly.

Realizing he'd broken a town ordinance forbidding the firing of a gun within the city limits, he and Clements escape through the window onto the roof of the hotel. Half dressed and drunk Hardin jumped down off the roof and hid in a haystack until morning, avoiding Hickok and the police. In the morning he stole a horse and made his escape.

The incident enhanced Hardin's reputation as the killer who'd shoot a man just for snoring. The truth is a lot less nasty. Couger was Hardin's friend, and his death was just a stupid accident. In Hardin's autobiography he described the impact of the incident on his reputation, *"They say I killed six or seven men for snoring. Well, it ain't true. I only killed one man for snoring."*

More gunfights and killings followed involving two Texas Special Policemen, three members of a negro-posse sent from Austin, a gunfight in Willis, and another Texas State Policeman in Hemphill.

**Sutton-Taylor Feud**
In 1872 Hardin was in Gonzales County where he married Jane Bowen and reconnected with his cousins who were allied with the Taylor family. The Taylors were having an

ongoing dispute with the Suttons. The dispute had been going on for years. In August of 1872 Hardin was severely wounded by Phil Sublett who shot him with a shotgun over losses incurred in a poker game at the Gates Saloon in Trinity, Texas. The shotgun pellets embedded in Hardin's kidney and it looked like he wasn't going to live. While recuperating Hardin decided to settle down and surrender to the local sheriff. Hardin was hoping for a fresh start but when he found out how many murders the sheriff was going to charge him with, he changed his mind. A relative smuggled a hacksaw into Hardin's jail cell, allowing him to cut through the window bars and make an escape.

Hardin then shot and killed two Sutton family supporters: first he killed Deputy Sheriff J. B. Morgan, and later that same day, Morgan's boss, County Sheriff Jack Helm. Hardin then helped his brother-in-law, Joshua Bowen, escape from jail. Bowen was being held on murder charges. Hardin, Bowen, and Bill and Jim Taylor then murdered Billy Sutton and Gabriel Slaughter. The body count was mounting, so Hardin escaped to Florida where he met up with his wife and daughter.

Back in Texas, Hardin reconnected with his pals at the Comanche Saloon to celebrate his twenty-first birthday. It's hard to believe that someone so young could have killed so many people. When Deputy Sheriff Charles Webb entered the saloon Hardin approached and asked if he was there to arrest him. Webb said no so Hardin invited him for a drink. What followed is unclear: Hardin claimed Webb went for his gun, while others say he was merely reaching for an arrest warrant for one of Hardin's friends. Someone shouted a warning, and a gunfight ensued, resulting in Webb's death.

**The Capture and Trial**

Texas Governor Richard B. Hubbard authorized a reward of $4,000 for Hardin's arrest. Hardin was hiding out near the Florida-Alabama border under the alias James W. Swain. Hardin's violent rampage continued with the wounding of a man trying to resolve a dispute between Hardin and another man, an arrest for having marked cards, the murder of a former slave, and the blinding of another. Hardin had numerous run-ins with former slaves, leading one to believe his Confederate slave-owner mentality lasted his whole life.

He was finally arrested by the Texas Rangers on a train in Pensacola, Florida. Again the details of the arrest are conflicting. Hardin claimed he was arrested while smoking a pipe, and that a Ranger found Hardin's pistol under his shirt. The Rangers claim Hardin tried to draw his gun, but it got tangled in his suspenders, after which, they knocked him out. It is a little hard to believe that a man who was so practiced a gunfighter would fumble in that manner, but if Wyatt Earp's cartridge belt could slip down around his legs while he was trying to mount his horse in the middle of a gunfight, I suppose anything is possible.

In June of 1878 Hardin was tried, convicted and sentenced to twenty-five years in jail for the murder of Deputy Sheriff Webb. Later he was also convicted of the murder of J. B. Morgan and given a two-year sentence to be served concurrently. After a number of attempts to escape,

Hardin finally accepted his fate, and spent his time studying the law and reading theological books, eventually becoming the superintendent of the prison's Sunday School.

Hardin's health deteriorated while he was in prison with one of his wounds becoming infected, forcing him to be bedridden for two years. Hardin may have killed numerous men, but he did not escape unscathed; he was wounded in the knee, the left thigh, right side, hip, elbow, shoulder, and back. In 1894, after seventeen years in prison, Hardin was released. His wife had died while he was in jail. On July 21st while back in Gonzales, Texas, Hardin passed the bar becoming a lawyer.

But Hardin just couldn't stay out of trouble. According to a newspaper article written in 1900, Hardin bet he could knock a man off a soapbox with one shot; he won the bet, but the man died from the fall. In El Paso, Hardin pistol-whipped lawman John Selman, Jr. over the arrest of Hardin's friend, a sometime-prostitute, M'Rose. Selman's father, also a former gunfighter and outlaw, responded by having heated words with Hardin. That evening Hardin went to the Acme Saloon to play dice. Around midnight Selman, Sr. entered the bar, approached Hardin from behind, and shot him in the head, killing him instantly. Selman then fired three more shots into Hardin making sure he was dead.

No one knows for sure how many men John Wesley Hardin, the preacher's son, actually killed, but whatever the number, it was a lot. Hardin was the prototypical western gunslinger with at least twenty-seven confirmed murders to his discredit, and perhaps as many as forty-two if unconfirmed accounts are added in. The southern preacher's son who became both a killer and lawyer is an enduring symbol of the American West, and the lingering legacy of a conflicted nation, forged out of a moral ambivalence towards solving problems with guns.

*"... you see what drink and passion will do. If you wish to be successful in life, be temperate and control your passions; if you don't, ruin and death is the result"* - John Wesley Hardin

**Billy The Kid**

# Henry *Billy The Kid* McCarty
## September 17th, 1859 – July 14th, 1881

*"I like to dance, but not in the air."* – Billy The Kid

**Henry McCarty**

Henry McCarty, better known as Billy The Kid, became synonymous with the vision of the western outlaw gunslinger despite the fact that he was born in New York City and never robbed a bank, train, or stagecoach. He did however kill eight or nine men, rustled cattle, and stole the occasional horse when necessary to make a quick getaway. Life in the semi-lawless frontier West was never as black and white as often portrayed. The so-called law was often as corrupt and murderous as the men they were hired to bring to justice. Outlaws often had as much support from the public as their badge-carrying adversaries. Murder was as frequently attributable to the economic avarice and political malfeasance of elected officials as it was to the belligerent behavior and drunken stupidity of the cowboys. Was Billy The Kid the crazed murderer portrayed in the dime novels, or was he like a lot of cowboys, a murderer, yes, but also a victim of circumstance and environment? McCarty's father died when he was very young, leaving his mother a widow. The family moved to Indianapolis where his mother met William Henry Harrison Antrim whom she eventually married. They then moved on to Wichita, Kansas, Santa Fe, New Mexico, and ultimately Silver City, New Mexico. In 1874 McCarty's mother died. He was fifteen years old and on his own.

His life of crime started shortly thereafter when he and a friend, George Schaefer, nicknamed Sombrero Jack, stole some clothes and two pistols from a local Chinese laundry. It was a minor offense with minimal punishment, but time in jail was not to the future desperado's liking, so he escaped captivity by climbing up the jailhouse chimney. McCarty developed his skills with a Winchester rifle and Colt revolver. He also became proficient in Spanish. A wanted poster of a few years later offered five thousand dollars for his capture. He was described as eighteen-years old, five foot, three inches tall, weighing one hundred and twenty-five pounds, with light hair, blue eyes, and even features.

## Kid Antrim

After a brief troubled stay with his stepfather William Antrim, he traveled on to the Arizona Territory where he spent his time gambling in saloons when he wasn't working as a ranch-hand for Henry Hooker. During this period McCarty befriended a former soldier and current criminal John R. Mackie. Together McCarty and Mackie stole horses from the soldiers in nearby Camp Grant. To hide his identity, McCarty used his stepfather's name becoming known as Kid Antrim.

In 1877 a local blacksmith bully, Francis *Windy* Cahill, started picking on McCarty, calling him names. While playing poker Cahill called McCarty a pimp. When McCarty responded by calling Cahill a son-of-a-bitch, a fight broke out with Cahill throwing the diminutive McCarty to the floor. The two men fought for McCarty's revolver with McCarty gaining control. McCarty shot and killed Cahill. McCarty is detained but manages to escape before the authorities arrive. He steals a horse and heads to the New Mexico Territory. On the way the Apaches take his horse forcing him to make his way on foot to Pecos Valley. Half dead, he arrives at the home of a friend John Jones, a member of the Seven Rivers Warriors. Jones mother nurses McCarty back to health. When he recovers McCarty joins the gang stealing cattle from cattle baron John Chisum. Around this time McCarty starts calling himself William H. Bonney. There's no reference as to why or where he came up with the name.

**The Lincoln County War**

McCarty got a job in Lincoln County, New Mexico, working as a ranch-hand for Englishman rancher, John Tunstall, and his partner, lawyer Alexander McSween. Tunstall and McSween had gone into direct competition with gunmen and business magnates Lawrence Murphy, James Dolan and John Riley. The Murphy group had a virtual economic and political monopoly on Lincoln County, and they weren't going to stand and watch

Tunstall break their stranglehold. The Murphy group used, their financial muscle to hire known outlaw gangs to harass Tunstall, and their political influence to protect and enforce their will.

McSween owed Dolan eight thousand dollars, and he wasn't in any hurry to pay it back. Dolan got a court order to attach forty thousand dollars worth of Tunstall's property and livestock in order to satisfy the debt. Sheriff William J. Brady, a Murphy supporter, assembled a large posse instructed to seize Tunstall's cattle. When Tunstall heard the Brady and his men were on his property he went out to intercept them. One of Brady's men shot Tunstall in what must have been a heated exchange. With Tunstall lying on the ground wounded in the chest another of Brady's men finished him off by putting a bullet in his head.

McCarty and Dick Brewer, Tunstall's foreman, were able to obtain murder warrants from the Lincoln County Justice of the Peace for Brady and his men for the killing of John

Tunstall. Brady arrested McCarty and Brewer, but U. S. Marshall Rob Widenmann ultimately set them free. Brewer then formed a group called the *Lincoln County Regulators* to combat Brady and Murphy's hired guns. The Regulators included McCarty, now calling himself Bonney, Doc Scurlock, Charlie Bowdre, and others. On March 9th, 1878 the Regulators captured and killed the two men, Frank Baker and William Morton, who were believed responsible for killing John Tunstall. The violence continued on both sides with numerous murders and killings including Dick Brewer, Sheriff Brady, and his deputy George Hindman. McCarty and two other Regulators were believed to have killed three men during these violent exchanges.

On Sunday July 14th, 1878, McSween and about fifty or sixty Regulators went into Lincoln and positioned themselves strategically throughout the town. The protection was needed to safeguard the McSween residence and a nearby bunkhouse. For the next five days there were intermittent shootings and standoffs. On July

Dirty Dave Rudabaugh

**Pat Garrett**

19th McSween gathered his men in his house. All hell broke out when Deputy Sheriff Jack Long and Buck Powell set fire to the residence. During the firefight McSween was shot and killed by Robert Beckwith. McCarty then killed Beckwith in revenge.

Something had to be done to put and end to the violence and chaos that was happening in Lincoln. On November 13th, 1878 the new Governor of New Mexico, Lew Wallace issued an amnesty proclamation pardoning anyone involved in the Lincoln County War since the date of John Tunstall's murder. The amnesty specifically excluded anyone that had been convicted of a crime or anyone that was currently under indictment. McCarty and three other Regulators were indicted for the murder of Mescalero Indian Agency bookkeeper Morris Bernstein. The charges were dropped for the other men but not McCarty. He appears to be specifically excluded by the authorities from the amnesty.

McCarty wrote Governor Wallace offering to testify against the men who brutally murdered Lincoln County lawyer Huston Chapman in exchange for the Governor granting him a pardon. Wallace agreed and McCarty surrendered to the authorities and provided a statement regarding Chapman's murder. Weeks passed and McCarty still languished in jail. He figured Wallace was going to renege on his promise so McCarty escaped and fled to Fort Sumner, New Mexico.

**The Joe Grant Gunfight**

McCarty stayed out of trouble until January 19th, 1880 when he shot and killed Joe Grant in the Hargrove Saloon, in Fort Sumner. What is interesting here is how the killing took place. It seems Grant was threatening to kill McCarty for some unknown reason, perhaps merely to enhance his reputation as the man that killed Billy The Kid, but nobody really knows for sure. It appears that McCarty was aware of Grant's intentions, so he approached Grant admiring his revolver. He asked to see it. For some strange reason Grant complies. When McCarty examines the gun, he sees it only had three shells in the chambers, he spins the cylinder so that it's lined up to fire the next shot on an empty chamber. He hands the gun back to Grant who then sticks the pistol in McCarty's face and pulls the trigger. When Grant's gun fails to fire, McCarty draws his pistol and shoots Grant in the head.

McCarty befriended rancher Jim Greathouse who introduced McCarty to Dirty Dave Rudabaugh, the same Rudabaugh that Wyatt Earp was after when he met Doc Holliday. McCarty, Rudabaugh, and Billy Wilson were hiding out at Greathouse's ranch. They were cornered by a posse led by Deputy Sheriff James Carlyle.

McCarty told Carlyle they were holding Greathouse hostage. Carlyle offered himself as a hostage in return for the freedom of Jim Greathouse. McCarty's group agrees and Carlyle is taken hostage, replacing Greathouse who may or may not have been a real hostage. When Carlyle tries to escape through a window, he is shot three times and killed. The posse withdrew and McCarty, Rudabaugh, and Wilson escaped. A few weeks later McCarty, Rudabaugh, Wilson, Tom Pickett, and fellow ex

Regulators, Charlie Bowdre, and Tom O'Folliard rode into Fort Sumner not knowing a posse led by Sheriff Pat Garrett was waiting for them. Garrett's men opened fire killing O'Folliard.

**The Capture and Escape**

On December 23rd, 1880, Garrett's posse finally caught up to the fugitives at Stinking Springs, killing Bowdre and capturing McCarty, Rudabaugh, Wilson, and Pickett. McCarty was taken to Santa Fe. He appealed to Governor Wallace for clemency but was denied. The trial took place in Mesilla, New Mexico. McCarty was found guilty of the murder of Sheriff William Brady and sentenced to hang. There were no other convictions for any of the participants in the Lincoln County War. But Billy The Kid wasn't quite finished yet.

McCarty was moved to Lincoln where he was held on the second floor of the courthouse awaiting execution. While on the way back from the outhouse McCarty manages to slip out of his handcuffs and overpower the deputy in charge. In the scuffle McCarty manages to get a hold of the deputy's gun. He shoots the fleeing deputy in the back, killing him. McCarty manages to get into Garrett's office where he retrieves a shotgun. He positioned himself on the top floor near a window waiting for the other deputy to respond to the gunshots. When the second deputy entered the street McCarty shoots and kills him. After murdering the two deputies McCarty steals a horse and escapes.

**Pat Garrett and The Kid**

Three months later, Garrett went back to Fort Sumner after hearing rumors that McCarty was in the area. On July 14th, 1881 Garrett went to question McCarty's friend Pete Maxwell. The two men were sitting in Maxwell's dimly lit bedroom when McCarty entered. McCarty didn't recognize Garrett in the darkened room so he asks *"Quien es? Quien es?"* (Who is it? Who is it?). Garrett recognizes McCarty's voice, so he draws his gun firing two shots. The first shot hits McCarty in the chest killing him instantly. Billy The Kid is dead.

When Garrett went to collect the reward for capturing Billy The Kid dead or alive, acting Governor William G.

Rich refused to pay. The citizens of Las Vegas, Mesilla, Santa Fe, and White Oaks raised a collection of seven thousand dollars when they heard Garrett wasn't being paid. A year after Billy The Kid's death, the New Mexico legislature passed an act granting Garrett the reward.

**Butch Cassidy**

## Robert Leroy, *Butch Cassidy*, Parker
## April 13th, 1866 – November 6th, 1909 [?]

*"Utah has no regrets over the loss of so energetic a citizen, but hopes the climate of Argentina will prove more soothing to the tingling nerves of Butch Cassidy than did the climate of this mountain region."*
- The Ogden Standard, February 21, 1910

Unlike many of the colorful characters of the Old West, Robert Leroy Parker's life wasn't shaped by the economic and social upheaval of the Civil War, but by a pair of overalls. Parker was the oldest of thirteen children to Maximilian Parker and Ann Campbell Gilles, British, Mormon immigrants that heeded the call of Brigham Young to settle in Utah. As a young teen Parker worked on various farms and ranches in order to earn money for the family. In 1880 he took the long trip into town in order to purchase a new pair of overalls, but by the time he got there, the store was closed. Parker broke into the store, took the overalls, and left a note saying he'd pay for the pants on his next visit. The storekeeper wasn't satisfied with Parker's IOU and pressed charges. Parker was arrested, tried, and found not guilty. Despite the verdict, the seemingly violent-averse friendly young man was left with an unhealthy distrust of the authorities and the legal system.

**The Nickname**

During this period Parker met his mentor, an old-time cowboy, rustler, and horse thief, John Tolliver McClammy, who went by the alias Mike Cassidy. Cassidy taught the young Parker how to shoot and train horses. In 1884 Parker left Utah to seek his fortune. He bounced around Colorado, Wyoming, and Montana, ending up in Telluride, Colorado. During this time Parker started calling himself Roy Cassidy, in honor of his old mentor. The Butch nickname came from Cassidy's brief employment as a butcher.

On June 24th, 1889 Cassidy and a few friends robbed the San Miguel Valley Bank in Telluride. After getting away with more than twenty thousand dollars Cassidy and his gang fled to Robbers Roost, a criminal hideout in southeastern, Utah. The following year Cassidy purchased a ranch in Dubois, Wyoming, close to the infamous Hole-In-the Wall outlaw hideout in the Big Horn Mountains of Johnston County, Wyoming. The area was a perfect hideout guarded by narrow passes making it impossible for anyone to get in without being detected. In 1884 Cassidy became involved with legendary female rancher Ann Bassett. If you want to learn more about Ann and Josie Basset and the girls of the Wild Bunch, check out *Organized Crime Queens, The Secret World of Female Gangsters*.

## The Basset Girls

The Bassett family ran a ranch that supplied outlaws on the run with fresh horses, supplies, and the companionship of the Bassett sisters, Ann and Josie. Cassidy served eighteen months of a two-year sentence for stealing horses and a running a protection racket for the local ranchers. After his release and pardon in 1896 he had a brief affair with Ann Bassett's older sister, Josie, before going back to Ann. As a side note there is some evidence

Allan Pinkerton

**Charlie Siringo**

that Ann Bassett and Etta Place, the girlfriend of the Sundance Kid (Harry Alonzo Longabaugh), were the same person. Although the evidence is speculative and inconclusive, it is nevertheless compelling. The two women were consistently described in the same way, with the same looks, manner, and character. The murky final histories of Cassidy, Longabaugh, and Etta Place, make for interesting conjecture.

**The Wild Bunch**

Although Cassidy and Sundance were friends and fellow members of the Wild Bunch, Cassidy's best friend was William Ellsworth *Elzy* Lay. The two met in 1889, when Lay was working on a ranch, possibly the Bassett ranch, in Browns Park, strategically located near the borders of Utah, Colorado, and Wyoming. Other members of the Wild Bunch other than Lay, Cassidy, and Sundance were *Kid Curry* Logan, Ben *The Tall Texan* Kilpatrick, Harry Tracy, Will *News* Carver, Laura Bullion, and George Curry. The Wild Bunch committed a series of robberies the most infamous being the June 2nd, 1899 robbery of the Union

Pacific Overland Flyer, creating quite a public stir and a massive manhunt that included professional killer and sometime detective Tom Horn and Pinkerton detective Charlie Siringo.

In July, Cassidy planned and help execute the robbery of the Colorado and Southern Railroad near Folsom, New Mexico. During the robbery, Lay shot and killed Sheriff Edward Farr and Henry Love. He was caught and sentenced to life in prison but was pardoned in 1906 after helping quell a prison riot. He died in 1934.

More robberies, shootouts, and killings followed. In December of 1900 Cassidy, Longabaugh, Logan, Kilpatrick, and Carver posed for the famous *Fort Worth Five Photograph*, a copy of which was used by the Pinkerton Detective Agency in wanted posters.

### Escape To South America

Things were getting too hot in the States. Will Carver had been killed, and Ben Kilpatrick and Laura Bullion had been captured and arrested. In 1901, Cassidy, Longabaugh, and

Etta Place fled to New York and then on the Buenos Aires. They purchased a ranch in Cholila, Argentina. In 1905 two English-speaking bandits robbed a bank seven hundred miles from Cholila.

Pinkerton agent Frank Dimaio discovered their hideout and was closing in. He already had the location, and he had obtained an arrest warrant from Governor Julio Lezana. Unfortunately for him, he was prevented from making the arrest due to the severe winter weather. Sheriff Edward Humphreys, a Welsh Argentinean was friends with Cassidy and had a crush on Etta Place, so he warned the outlaws the Pinkertons were close. Cassidy and friends sold the ranch and fled to Chile. Cassidy, Longabaugh and another outlaw snuck across the border to Argentina and robbed the Banco de Nacion before heading back to Chile. Etta Place was tired of life on the run, so on June 30th, 1906 she and Longabaugh made their way back to the States, landing in San Francisco, while Cassidy got a job guarding the payroll at the Concordia Tin Mine in Bolivia. When Longabaugh returned, the two friends traveled to the frontier town of Santa Cruz, Bolivia.

## The Legend Is Created

On November 4th, 1908 near Tupiza, in southern Bolivia two men robbed the payroll being transported to the Aramayo Mine. Three days later villagers in San Vicente became suspicious of two English-speaking visitors and reported them to the military. When the soldiers arrived a shootout took place with both suspects killed. According to records when the bodies were examined their actual deaths appeared to be a murder-suicide. Both men had been badly injured with at least one of them so severely wounded that his death was imminent. It appeared one of the men shot and killed his partner in order to put him out of misery. He then shot himself to avoid capture.

There were other American outlaws in the area, who like Cassidy and Longabaugh fled the States to South America. There is no evidence the two dead robbers were actually Butch and Sundance, nevertheless they were the most high profile American outlaws in the general area. The 1969 movie, *Butch Cassidy and the Sundance Kid*, perpetuated the myth that Cassidy and Sundance died in the Bolivian shootout, however rumors and anecdotal evidence persisted that the two men killed weren't Parker and Longabaugh. In a 1960 interview Josie Bassett claimed that Cassidy, using the alias *Johnnie Nevada*, came to visit her in the 1920s and that he lived until 1945. Researchers eventually got permission to exhume the two bodies buried in the San Vicente cemetery. After analysis, it was determined the remains were not Robert Leroy Parker and Harry Alonzo Longabaugh.

Questions remain: what really happened to Parker and Longabaugh, and was Etta Place, who disappeared in 1909, really Ann Bassett who died in 1956? No one really knows.

The Sundance Kid

## Harry Alonzo 'Sundance Kid' Longabaugh
## Sometime in 1867 – November 6th, 1909

> *"Harry Longabaugh, Cassidy's right hand and leading lieutenant, is almost as dangerous in criminal courage and intellect as the great Butch himself."*
> – Rosebud County News, May 15th, 1902

Most of the details of Harry Alonzo Longabaugh's life as the Sundance Kid and his involvement in the Wild Bunch have been covered in the discussion of Butch Cassidy. There are however several interesting items relating to Longabaugh that you may find interesting. Longabaugh was born in Mont Clare, Pennsylvania. When he was fifteen, he left home with his cousin to seek his fortune out West.

It seems that amongst the more practical qualities required to be part of the Wild Bunch, it was also helpful to have a cool nickname. Butch Cassidy as already mentioned was dubbed Butch based on his short-lived career as a butcher. Will *News* Carver received his handle based on his fondness for reading about himself in the newspapers. Ben *The Tall Texan* Kilpatrick was tall and from Texas. Tom *Black Jack* Ketchum was once mistaken for another outlaw *Black Jack* Christian and the nickname just stuck. Harvey *Kid Curry* Logan adopted his nickname from a friend *Flat Nose* George Curry who was also a member of the Wild Bunch. In Longabaugh's case he adopted the *nom de plum* from his eighteen-month stay in a Sundance, Wyoming jail for stealing a gun, horse, and saddle.

Make no mistake, the Wild Bunch were violent criminals, and although both Cassidy and the Sundance Kid preferred to avoid gunplay, when necessary they were definitely up to the task. Sundance did have a reputation that he was fast on the draw, but the fact remains there is only one confirmed incident where he wounded two lawmen in a posse that attempted to raid their Hole-In-The-Wall hideout. The newspapers at the time wrote of murders committed by *The Kid*; murders mistakenly attributed to the Sundance Kid when in fact they were committed by fellow gang member Kid Curry.

The most intriguing aspect of the legend of the Sundance Kid is not so much his life but the mystery surrounding his assumed death in Bolivia. A variety of stories have surfaced regarding what really happened to Butch, Sundance, and Sundance's longtime girlfriend Etta Place, who apparently disappeared off the face of the earth in 1909. Over the years many frauds have come forward claiming to be both Butch Cassidy and the Sundance Kid, but none survived the harsh scrutiny of historians. To me, the most compelling facts that point to the two outlaws surviving are the lack of confirming DNA evidence when the San Vicente bodies were exhumed and examined; the report that Josie Basset, an intimate friend of both men, claimed to have been visited by Cassidy in the 1920s; and the odd disappearance of Etta Place soon after her lovers were assumed dead. Did Harry Alonzo Longabaugh and his friend Robert Leroy Parker die in Bolivia? I have no idea, but their potential survival does make for a fascinating legend. And what happened to Etta Place?

**Cole Younger**

## Thomas Coleman *Cole* Younger
### January 15th, 1844 – March 21st, 1916

*"We tried a desperate game and lost. But we are rough men used to rough ways, and we will abide by the consequences."*
– Cole Younger

Cole Younger and his brothers are best known as members of the James-Younger Gang, a group that included the notorious Jesse James and his brother Frank. Cole Younger's life like many of the villains and heroes of the Old West was shaped by The Civil War. Younger's father was a successful Missouri farmer and slave owner that supported the Union during the war. Although Missouri did not enter the war, the population's sympathies tended to be mostly leaning to the Confederacy, and that put Missourians in direct conflict with their neighbors, the pro-Union, free-state Kansas Jayhawkers. The result was the Kansas-Missouri Border War, a nasty guerrilla affair that pitted the pro-Union Jayhawkers against the pro-Confederate Bushwhackers led by William Quantrill and his raiders.

Although Younger's father was a slave owner, he backed the Union as he felt that the North would prevail in the War and that slavery would be abolished. Unfortunately despite his Union leanings, he still ended up being killed by a detachment of Union militiamen in 1862. Before his father's death Cole was already rebelling against the frequent Jayhawker raids by joining William Quantrill's raiders, but after his father's murder Cole was pushed over the edge. He participated in the vicious attack on Lawrence, Kansas that claimed two hundred lives. The town was looted and burned. Cole left Quantrill's Raiders and joined the regular Confederate army earning the rank of Captain. After the War, Cole returned home to find his family farm in ruins.

Post-war Missouri was controlled by militant Unionist Radicals. A new state constitution barred southern sympathizers from voting, serving on juries, or holding public office. The resentments created by the war and its aftermath pushed a lot of men like Cole Younger, and fellow Missourians Jesse and Frank James, into lives of crime. On February 13th, 1866 the James-Younger Gang robbed the Clay County Savings Association in Liberty, Missouri, taking in a haul of sixty thousand dollars. Over the next few years the James-Younger Gang robbed twelve banks, seven trains, and four stagecoaches, killing eleven innocent people. The end of Younger's criminal career came in 1876 when the gang failed in their attempt to rob a bank in Northfield, Minnesota.

Bob Younger, Jesse and Frank James entered the bank while Cole and the rest of the gang controlled the street. When the bank clerk, Joseph Lee Heywood refused to open the vault he was shot and killed. Assistant Cashier, Alonzo Enos Bunker was shot in the shoulder while trying to escape.

The townsfolk hearing the gunshots went and got their guns. A shootout ensued with several of the outlaws killed. Cole was wounded in the thigh. During the escape the gang split up with the James' brothers going off on their own. The posse that went after them finally caught up to the Younger faction near Madelia, Minnesota. Cole, Jim, and Bob Younger were tried, found guilty, and sentenced to twenty-five years in prison. Bob Younger died in prison of tuberculosis in 1889; Jim Younger was paroled in 1901 but committed suicide the next year. Cole was also paroled in 1901. After his release from prison Cole wrote his memoir and toured in *The Cole Younger and Frank James Wild West Company*. Cole Younger justified his criminal behavior as an avenging Confederate guerrilla. The residue of Cole Younger's resentment can still be seen in today's political, social, and regional animosity.

**Jesse James**

# Jesse Woodson James
## September 5th, 1847 – March 4th, 1868

*"Bob Ford I don't trust; I think he is a sneak; but Charlie Ford is as true as steel."*

– Jesse James

When times are bad or when society is in upheaval villains often become folk heroes; this is the case of Jesse James, but Jesse Woodson James was no hero, he was a vicious killer and outlaw. The idea that he was some kind of Old West Robin Hood is nonsense; Jesse James the folk hero was a product of good public relations, a sympathetic, pro-Confederate, Missouri audience, and a news media eager to profit from common criminals that justified their behavior as revenge for the evils of the Kansas-Missouri border wars.

Jesse, his older brother Frank, and his younger sister Susan were born in Clay County Missouri, an area dubbed Little Dixie, as it was settled by southern pro slave farmers.

Their father was a Baptist preacher who helped found William Jewell College in Liberty, Missouri. He was a prosperous farmer with six slaves and one hundred acres of farmland. His preaching took him to California where he died when Jesse was only three years old. Jesse's mother married two more times eventually settling with Dr. Reuben Samuel in 1855.

**Pro Confederate Sympathies**

Missouri was a border state and although the population consisted of both pro-North and pro-South sympathizers, the vast majority, seventy-five percent, were transplanted southerners, with Clay County predominantly southern in attitude and economics. Although only ten percent of the population in Missouri were slaves, in Clay County, the slave population was twenty-five per cent. Pro-slavery Missourians moved to Kansas to influence the future of slavery in Kansas. The result was a vicious and deadly border war between the pro-Confederate Missourian guerrillas called the *Bushwhackers*, and the pro-Union militias called the *Jayhawkers*.

**The Border Wars**

Both sides committed atrocities with many innocent people killed. The James-Samuel family sided with the Confederates making them a target of the Kansas pro-Union militias. In May of 1863 their farm was attacked. Reuben Samuel was hung from a tree but survived. Jesse was beaten and lashed. Frank James escaped and joined Quantrill's Raiders and participated in the massacre of two hundred people in the abolitionist center of Lawrence, Kansas. In 1864, young Jesse joined his older brother Frank as a Quantrill guerrilla under the command of Fletch Taylor. After Taylor was wounded, the James brothers joined another guerrilla group under the command of Bloody Bill Anderson. The James brothers reportedly participated in the Centralia Massacre that resulted in twenty-two unarmed Union soldiers being executed, with some being scalped and dismembered. They were also involved in the defeat and execution of one hundred surrendered Union troops including their commander, Major A.V.E. Johnson. As a result of Frank and Jesse's activities, the rest of the family was forced to move to

Nebraska. When Bloody Bill Anderson was killed Frank and Jesse separated. Frank followed Quantrill into Kentucky while Jesse followed Archie Clement into Texas. During these battles Jesse suffered two severe chest wounds.

**The James-Younger Gang**
When the war ended, Missouri was bitterly divided between anti-slavery Republicans, segregationist Democrats, and pro-slavery ex-Confederates. The Missouri Republican, Reconstruction administration freed the slaves, and passed a new state constitution severely limiting the civil rights of pro-Confederate sympathizers, temporarily restricting them from voting, sitting on juries, becoming corporate officers, or preaching. The war may have been over, but the hatred, desire for revenge, and instinct for violence remained.

While Jesse recovered from his chest wounds, his ex commander, Archie Clement, continued his bushwhacker activities against the Republican regime. He is credited with the first peacetime bank robbery in Liberty, Missouri, on February 13th, 1866. Former Republican militia officers owned the bank. True to form, the gang killed an innocent college student during their escape. It is unclear whether the James brothers were involved in this robbery but on June 13th, 1866, they appear to have taken part in the murder of a jailer while freeing captured members of Quantrill's gang. Governor Fletcher ordered a company of militia to put an end to the continued violence. Archie Clement was ultimately shot and killed by the state militia.

What was left of the politically motivated Clement gang, including the James brothers, became common criminals, robbing small local banks and killing anyone that got in their way. Any justification relating to war, politics, or economics was pure fiction except perhaps in their own minds. In 1868 Jesse and Frank joined up with the Younger brothers to rob a bank in Russellville, Kentucky.

Jesse's reputation gained traction when he mistakenly murdered the bank cashier, John Sheets, during the robbery of the Daviess County Saving Association, thinking he was Samuel Cox, the man that killed Bloody Bill Anderson. The robberies, murders and daring escapes made for sensational must-read newspaper reports. Jesse James was now publicly named an outlaw with a reward on his head. Up until this point James was just another murdering criminal thug, but his reputation began to change with his new association with the founder and editor of the Kansas City Times, John Newman Edwards. Edwards a Confederate and secessionist sympathizer published a series of letters from James proclaiming his innocence and pushing the Southern party line. Edwards used James letters and the accompanying editorials to turn Jesse James, the common criminal, into Jesse James, the embodiment of Confederate resistance.

Jesse James became the face of the James-Younger gang and together the two sets of brothers and their ex-guerrilla partners robbed banks and stagecoaches throughout the Midwest. On July 21st, 1873 wearing Ku Klux Klan masks, the gang derailed and robbed the Rock Island train in Adair, Iowa. The racist bigotry symbolized by the wearing of the KKK masks should end any romantic notion one might have had for what amounts to nothing more than a gang of miserable murdering miscreants. Few Western legends were completely innocent; but the James and Younger brothers were not lawmen like the Earps, nor were they ranchers like the Clantons, they were just thieves and killers.

**The Pinkerton Detective Agency**
The robberies and murders where piling up. The pro-Confederate press was pushing Jesse James false Robin Hood persona, and the gang was receiving widespread protection from Southern-leaning locals. It was time for the Pinkerton National Detective Agency from Chicago to be brought into the picture.

The Pinkerton Detective Agency run by Allan Pinkerton was no paragon of virtue or upholder of justice. His detectives were little more than hired guns, men like Tom Horn, employed to break union strikes for corporate clients, or resolve land disputes by any means necessary in favor of the regional economic powers that hired them. Pinkerton detectives were often substituted for real lawmen in order to combat the lawlessness that characterized the post Civil War settling of the West. A number of agents were sent to capture the James and Younger brothers but they all turned up dead. On the evening of January 25th, 1875 Pinkerton agents firebombed the James-Samuel family home killing Jesse's half brother Archie and maiming Zerelda Samuel, Jesse's mother. A James neighbor, Daniel Askew, was killed because he was suspected of co-operating with the detectives. The raid was a disaster, almost leading to an amnesty for the James and Younger brothers from the Missouri state legislature.

**The Northfield, Minnesota Blunder**

As described earlier in the Cole Younger section, the gang tried to rob the First National Bank of Northfield, Minnesota. The cashier refused to open the safe and was killed; and the assistant cashier was shot in the shoulder trying to escape. The townspeople heard the shots and a gun battle ensued with two of the gang killed and several more wounded. Another innocent bystander, Nicholas Gustafson was also killed during the skirmish. A posse was put together to track down the gang. The James and Younger brothers split up, with the James brothers escaping to Missouri. The posse caught up with the Younger group killing one of their gang members, Charlie Pitts, and arresting Cole, Jim, and Bob Younger who were all tried, convicted, and sentenced to twenty-five years in prison.

**A Violent End for A Violent Killer**

Frank and Jesse laid low for three years living in Nashville, Tennessee under assumed names, but in 1879 they formed a new gang and started on a fresh robbery spree. Unlike the motivated battle-hardened guerrillas that formed the original gang, the new group was just a bunch of criminals without the slightest political justification that at least in part drove the original group.

In 1881 Jesse moved back to Missouri where he felt the locals would protect him, nevertheless he was becoming justifiably paranoid. Frank moved to Virginia where he figured he'd be safer. The gang was basically eliminated except for Jesse, Charlie Ford, and his brother Robert. Jesse asked the Ford brothers to move in with him for protection, but Jesse didn't trust Robert Ford. His concerns were justified. Ford had secretly cut a deal with Missouri Governor Thomas T. Crittenden to capture the infamous outlaw in return for a five thousand dollar reward put up by the railroad and express companies. Ford later stated he felt Jesse was on to him. He worried he'd be killed before he had a chance to do the same to Jesse. On April 3rd, 1882, while Jesse James was standing on a chair dusting a picture frame, Robert Ford shot him in the back of the head. Jesse James was dead.

In a bizarre example of mock justice designed to appease the locals, the Ford brothers were charged with first degree murder, however, they were quickly indicted, pleaded guilty, sentenced to death, and granted a pardon by Governor Crittenden all in one day. The Fords only received a small portion of the reward that was promised. Charlie Ford committed suicide in 1884 after developing tuberculosis and an addiction to morphine. On June 8th, 1892 Edward O'Kelley, carrying a double-barreled shotgun, walked into the Creede, Colorado saloon operated by Robert Ford, and shot Ford in the throat killing him instantly. Kelley was sentenced to life in prison but the sentence was commuted due to public sentiment. He was pardoned by the governor in 1902.

Jesse James was a vigilante, rebel, terrorist, murderer, and common criminal who justified his violent career as the actions of a Southern Confederate patriot. The fact is, Jesse James was a gangster who found stealing and murder to be more rewarding that working a farm. He was not a romantic figure nor was his actions politically defensible. Perceived injustices and economic necessity were mere excuses to justify his violent blood lust.

**Luke Short**

# Luke Short

## January 22, 1854 – September 8th, 1893

*"Luke was a little fellow, so to speak, about five feet, six inches in height, and weighing in the neighborhood of one hundred and forty pounds. It was a small package, but one of great dynamic force."*
– W. R. (Bat) Masterson, 1907

Luke Short had an interesting life, albeit relatively short, but considering he was in at least three famous gunfights it's amazing he survived to die of Bright's disease (chronic nephritis) rather than by Colt .45 induced lead poisoning. Short was a gunfighter, U. S. Army Scout, dispatch rider, faro dealer, gambler, boxing promoter, racehorse enthusiast, and saloon owner. For whatever reason he always seemed to be associated with the most famous people, places, and events of the era.

Short was a rough, uneducated cowboy making a living trading cheap "Pine Top" whiskey to the Sioux for buffalo hides, an activity that did not please the Sioux chiefs or the military. Having worn out his welcome in Nebraska and Dakota, Short found himself in Leadville, a Colorado mining boom town where he learned how to dress like a gentleman and gamble like a professional. His reputation as a well-liked fellow not to be trifled with was cemented when he shot a rival gambling opponent in the face who made the mistake of thinking he could outdraw him.

According to his friend Bat Masterson, people continually underestimated the speed and virtuosity of Short's ability with a pistol. He was dealing faro at the Oriental Saloon managed at the time by Wyatt Earp when Short and Charlie Storm got into a disagreement. Storm was a gambler and killer who had out-dueled his share of gunfighters. According to Masterson, Storm slapped Short, and both men went for their guns, but Masterson stepped in to calm the situation. He convinced Storm to go back to his room and cool off, but a few minutes later he confronted Short on the sidewalk while he was talking to Masterson. He grabbed Short knocking him off the sidewalk while at the same time going for his gun; but like others, he underestimated his opponent's ability. Short was faster on the draw putting a bullet in Storms head at close range. As Storm was falling, Short put another bullet in him making sure there'd be no response.

At different times, Short owned interests in three of the most famous saloons in the Old West: the Oriental in Tombstone, the White Elephant in Fort Worth, and the Longbranch in Dodge City. Short was a good friend of both Bat Masterson and Wyatt Earp, who together created the *Dodge City Peace Commission*. The Commission was a group of prominent gunfighters formed for the sole purpose of forcing the Mayor to allow Short back in town after he was run out of Dodge for playing music in the Longbranch Saloon contrary to a city ordinance. Despite Short's newly acquired stylish, sartorial appearance his cowboy background made him extremely popular and able to relate to his customers making the Longbranch the most popular saloon in Dodge. This did not please the Mayor who owned the neighboring saloon.

# The Dodge City Police Commission
## Will Harris, Luke Short, Bat Masterson, William Petillon
## Charlie Bassett, Wyatt Earp, Frank McLain, Neil Brown

Both bars had bands that played music, a popular feature in both establishments. The Mayor had an ordinance passed outlawing music in the bars. When Short was told about the new ordinance, he complied immediately, but the Mayor didn't. When Short heard the Mayor was still playing music in his place, he reinstated the band. The band was arrested and jailed. Short approached a police officer seeking bail for his employees, but the officer shot at him missing. Short returned fire but also missed. The exchanged resulted in Short being put on a train out of town and told not to come back.

Short wasn't going to let this stand. He contacted his friend Bat Masterson and together they put together a group of gunfighters led by Wyatt Earp. The Dodge City Peace Commission casually drifted into town. The Mayor got nervous when he heard Earp was in town with a group of gunfighters looking to reinstall Short. The Mayor approached Earp to resolve the problem without bloodshed. Earp negotiated a preliminary agreement. Short and Masterson then arrived for a more substantial meeting where Short insisted all his demands be met. The Mayor and the city fathers all agreed. Short was back in business thanks to what became known as the Dodge City Peace Commission, led by Short, Masterson, and Earp.

Despite the bloodless moral victory, Short tired of Dodge City politics and decided to sell his interest in the Longbranch. He made his way down to Fort Worth, Texas where he became a partner in the White Elephant Saloon, the fanciest, most costly saloon in the Southwest. Luke soon found that owning a saloon always seemed to lead to trouble.

At the center of the trouble was a dangerous gunfighter named Jim Courtright who had already killed a couple of men in Fort Worth and a couple more in New Mexico. According to Bat Masterson's account, Short knew Courtright all too well. When Courtright approached Short for a job as a bouncer in the White Elephant, Short declined his request. People in town were afraid of Courtright and Short worried his presence would scare off customers. Other accounts put a slightly different spin on the situation. Courtright's request for employment was nothing more than a veiled protection racket and Short wasn't going to be bullied.

It didn't take long after being denied employment that Courtright confronted Short in the lobby of the White Elephant. After a brief exchange of words Courtright went for his gun, but like others before him, he underestimated Short's ability. Short outdrew his attacker quickly putting five bullets in him before he fell lifeless to the ground.

Although Short started out life as an uneducated ruffian who sold whiskey to the Sioux, by the time he died he was a personable, well-read, respected married sporting gentleman.

**Elfego Baca**

# Elfego Baca

## February 10th, 1865 – August 27th, 1945

*"Elfego was, and is, controversial. He drank too much; talked too much ... he had a weakness for wild women. He was often arrogant and, of course, he showed no compunction about killing people."*

– Leon Metz, *The Shooters*

Elfego Baca was a lawman, lawyer, and politician in Socorro, New Mexico. His father was the marshal in Belen, New Mexico, and Baca wanted to follow in his footsteps and become a peace officer, so at the age of nineteen he deputized himself. The region was mostly lawless, dominated by cowboys that had little regard for rules in general, and the law in particular. They would drink, carouse, and harass the townsfolk with impunity, and that didn't sit well with the young Baca.

**The Frisco Shootout**

In 1884 in Middle San Francisco Plaza in Reserve, New Mexico, self-appointed Deputy Baca arrested a drunken cowboy, Charlie McCarty. McCarty's pals tried to retake their friend but Baca resisted by opening fire. He shot one man in the knee and the horse of another. The horse fell landing on its rider killing him. The dead cowboy was local rancher, Jon Slaughter's foreman.

When the matter went to court, the Justice of the Peace set McCarty free. Baca was unhappy with the verdict so he fled the courtroom still in possession of McCarty's gun. He took refuge in the adobe *jacal* of Geronimo Armijo. Bert Hearne, a Spur Lake rancher was sent to collect Baca by the Justice of the Peace to answer for the murder of Jon Slaughter's foreman. Baca refused to come out so Hearne broke down the door but Baca shot him in the stomach killing him.

At least forty cowboys, Baca later said it was eighty, surrounded the house and started firing. Over four thousand rounds were fired into the house but none hit Baca. The floor of the house was sunken below ground level allowing Baca to escape the onslaught unscathed. A number of the cowboy attackers weren't so lucky. Baca killed four of his attackers, wounding another eight. After thirty-three hours of mayhem Baca finally surrendered. Baca was arrested and tried for the murder of the foreman and Bert Hearne. During the trial Baca's attorney presented as evidence the door from the adobe *jacal* complete with over four hundred bullet holes, as well as false documentation stating Baca had been officially deputized when in fact he was self-appointed. Baca was acquitted, and the incident went down in history as the Frisco Shootout, establishing Baca's reputation as a badass defender of the law, or at least, the law as he saw it.

Eventually Baca became the official Sheriff of Socorro County. His reputation was such that wanted men were sent letters stating that if they didn't turn themselves in, he would assume they were resisting arrest and he would shoot them on sight. Most of those that received these letters surrendered peacefully. In 1888 Baca became a U. S. Marshal. In 1894 he was admitted to the bar as a lawyer.

Baca held a number of public offices including school superintendent, county clerk, district attorney, and mayor. During the Mexican Revolution Baca served as the official U. S. Representative of the Victoriano Huerta government. During this period Baca was charged with masterminding the escape of Mexican General José Inés Salazar from an Albuquerque jail, but he was found not guilty. When New Mexico became a state Baca ran for congress but lost; he remained a valued political operative able to turnout the Hispanic vote while working for Senator Bronson Cutting as a political investigator.

Baca was a colorful character whose legend was enhanced by his numerous achievements, exploits, and self-promotion. He supposedly once stole the gun of infamous Mexican revolutionary Pancho Villa, but that is likely another of the Baca's legendary fabled embellishments. As a lawyer Baca is said to have defended thirty men charged with murder with only one ever-serving time in jail. It is said he once received a telegram from El Paso, Texas, *"Need you at once. Have been charged with murder."* Baca responded with *"Leaving at once with three eyewitnesses."*

**Bass Reeves**

# PART II

# THE BLACK COWBOYS

The Civil War, like all wars, created its share of lost souls whose lives were altered by the political, economic, and psychological disruption caused by the conflict. This post war dislocation of soldiers combined with a push West from adventurous easterners, and immigrants looking for a better life, created a whole new set of conflicts pitting lawless wanderers, political aspirants, and economic interests against one another.

The war depleted the eastern supply of beef, creating a demand for the long-horned cattle that roamed the South West. Moving the cattle across the country was a monumental task that required tough, hard-nosed men who were willing to do a grueling job under harsh conditions. Civil War veterans, adventurers, ex slaves, natives, and Mexicans combined to fill the cowboy population. About one third of the cowboys were black.

### Bass Reeves

*"Eighty miles west of Fort Smith was known as 'the dead line,' and whenever a deputy marshal from Fort Smith or Paris, Texas, crossed the Missouri, Kansas & Texas track he took his own life in his hands and he knew it. On nearly every trail would be found posted by outlaws a small card warning certain deputies that if they ever crossed the dead line, they would be killed. Reeves has a dozen of these cards which were posted for his special benefit. And in those days such a notice was no idle boast, and many an outlaw has bitten the dust trying to ambush a deputy on these trails."*

- Oklahoma City newspaper article, 1907

### July 1838 – January 10th, 1910

Bass Reeves was born a slave in 1838 probably in Crawford County, Arkansas. Reports state he was owned by Colonel

George R. Reeves, but since Colonel Reeves was born in 1826, it's more likely he was originally owned by Reeves' parents William Steel Reeves and Nancy Totty Reeves. Colonel Reeves was a tax collector, state representative, commissioned Confederate officer, and ultimately Speaker of the House (Texas). Reeves County, Texas is named in his honor.

Little is known about Bass's early life, but he ultimately escaped slavery by fleeing into Indian Territory, supposedly after a card game with Colonel Reeves that ended in a fistfight. Indian Territory was a no-man's-land, off limits for everybody but Native Americans and outlaws. Lawmen were warned that crossing the Dead Line into the territory would end with their certain death. He learned his way around the badlands, as well as various native languages, while living with the Creek and Seminole nations.

During the Civil War, he served in the Union Indian Home Guard Regiment. When the war ended Bass became a farmer but his ability to speak several native languages and his knowledge of the territory made him a valuable guide for the Deputy U. S. Marshals that worked out of the Federal court in Fort Smith, Arkansas. Bass's guide experience served him well enough that hanging judge, Isaac C. Parker, appointed him one of the first, if not the first, black Deputy U. S. Marshals.

He served as Deputy Marshal for three decades supposedly capturing some three thousand criminals, gunning down at least a dozen. He was so confident of success he traveled his Oklahoma circuit with a cook, a wagon, and a sidekick lawman. His most notorious case was the time he went after his own son for murdering his wife. After being captured, his son was tried, convicted, and sentenced to life imprisonment, proving that for Bass, no one was above the law.

**Ned Huddleston**

## Ned Huddleston (Isom Dart)

### 1849 – 1900

If it weren't for the fact Ned Huddleston was black, he would probably be as famous as any of the well-known characters of the Old West. He crossed paths with many of the infamous legends we know well, people like Robert Leroy Parker (Butch Cassidy), Harry Alonzo Longabaugh (the Sundance Kid), Ann Bassett, and unfortunately as you will find out, gunslinger, Tom Horn.

Huddleston appeared to be every bit the post Civil War outlaw, standing six-foot, two-inches tall wearing his flat brimmed cowboy hat, flared-waist jacket, and sporting two backwards pointing six shooters at the waist. And what kind of legend could he be without an alias or two: *Isom Dart, the Black Fox,* and *the Calico Cowboy.*

Huddleston was born a slave in 1849. At the age of twelve he accompanied his Confederate officer owner to Texas for the Civil War. When the war was over, he was freed. He made his way down to the southern Texas-Mexican border where he found work as a rodeo clown, stunt rider, and expert horseman.

For a while he mined gold and silver but quit after being cheated out of his share by his partner. After an affair with a Shoshone woman in 1875, he teamed up with a Mexican bandit named Terresa. Together they survived rustling cattle and stealing horses as members of the Tip Gault Gang. The gang came to a nasty end one night while burying one of its members that died from being kicked by a horse, not an uncommon experience.

The Tip Gault outlaws were ambushed by an unhappy rancher that didn't appreciate their activities. All the members of the gang were killed except for Huddleston who jumped into the grave they were digging to hide. When the coast was clear, he crawled out and made it on foot to a nearby ranch where he stole a horse to make his escape. Unfortunately the rancher was able to get off a shot wounding Huddleston in the leg. Huddleston did manage to getaway, but exhausted and weak from blood loss he collapsed and fell off the horse.

He lay unconscious on the trail until he was found by *Billy Buck* Tittsworth. Tittsworth and Huddleston were pals when they were kids back in Arkansas. He lived on the neighboring plantation. Titttsworth patched up Huddleston enough so he could make his way out of the Brown's Hole area. In 1890 he changed his name to Isom Dart and returned to the area known as the birthplace of Ann and Josie Bassett, ranchers, outlaws, and Wild Bunch girlfriends. Ann and Jose Bassett ran a successful ranch that acted as a stopping off point for the Wild Bunch when they were on the run.

The Bassetts would supply the gang with fresh horses, supplies, and female companionship. Butch Cassidy's gang had five females that they trusted, Laura Bullion: a full-fledged member of the gang; Maude Davis: Butch Cassidy's best friend's Elzy Lay's wife; Etta Place: the Sundance Kid's girlfriend; and the two Bassett girls, Ann and Josie. There are those that think, and there is some evidence to support the idea, that the elusive and mysterious Etta Place was really Ann Bassett.

Ned Huddleston was now known as Isom Dart. He owned a ranch in the area and was accused by some of the large cattle barons led by Ora Haley of stocking his herd by stealing cattle. This accusation was not made in a vacuum. The Bassets were also accused of stealing cattle along with fellow small ranchers Matt Rash and Jim McKnight. There seemed to have been a continuous tit-for-tat battle that went on between the small ranchers and their cattle baron neighbors. The large ranch operators were determined to drive the small guys out of business so they could take over their spreads. No one involved was innocent as far as the rustling went, but the big operations were definitely motivated by greed.

The Swan Land and Cattle Company hired notorious gunslinger Tom Horn to rid the area of these small ranches on the pretext of stamping out the cattle rustling. Horn was a killer who operated under the guise of a Pinkerton agent and ranch detective. Horn was supposedly hired to investigate and gather evidence of cattle rustling on Matt Rash who ran the Brown's Park Cattle Association. Horn went undercover as Tom Hicks and began working on Rash's ranch so he could gather proof. Once he had the evidence, he left a note for Rash to pack up and leave in sixty days. Rash ignored the warnings. Horn was authorized to kill Rash. He entered Rash's cabin and shot him at point-blank range. Before Rash died, he tried unsuccessfully to write the name of his killer.

Horn left the Bassett girls alone. Rumor had it he was going to marry Ann Bassett. One assumes that meant they had an affair which has a ring of truth to it as she basically slept her way through the Wild Bunch; but since she was the one to point a finger at Horn for Rash's murder, I'm not sure I buy it. It seems more likely Horn knew of the Bassett's relationship with the Wild Bunch, so instead of going after the Bassetts, he aimed his sights on the black man, Isom Dart, whom most people recognized as the former outlaw Ned Huddleston.

Horn set up an ambush by hiding under a pine tree near Dart's cabin. On October 3rd, 1900, Dart stepped out the front door of his cabin and was greeted by a bullet from Tom Horn's gun.

**William Pickett**

## William (Bill) Pickett
## December 5th, 1870 – April 2nd, 1932

Another black cowboy, Bill Pickett, is credited with inventing 'bulldogging' a staple of today's modern rodeo, but today's version is slightly different from what it was back in Pickett's day. Today's bulldogging has a cowboy chasing down a steer on horseback, jumping off the horse, grabbing the steer by the horns, and twisting it to the ground. Back in Pickett's time the cowboy did essentially the same thing except when he twisted the steer's neck towards him, he'd bite the animal's upper lip while raising his hands in the air. Not the kind of thing PETA would be thrilled seeing.

Pickett was your quintessential rodeo cowboy, expert in roping, riding, and bulldogging. Because he was black he wasn't allowed to compete against white cowboys so he and his four brothers created *The Pickett Brothers Bronco Busters and Rough Riders Association*. They traveled throughout the Southwest performing passing the hat for donations. In 1910 he performed as *The Dusky Demon* alongside Buffalo Bill Cody, Tom Mix, Will Rogers, and Bee Ho Gray in the *101 Ranch Wild West Show* that toured throughout the USA, Canada, Mexico, South America, and even England, Because of the racism of the time he often had to claim he was Comanche just so he could perform. Pickett was also the first black cowboy movie star appearing in the 1921 movies *The Bull-Dogger* and *The Crimson Skull*.

Like Josie Bassett, Pickett's death was at the hand, or rather the hoof of a horse. In 1932 Pickett died from injuries he sustained from a kick in the head by a horse. In 1972 he was posthumously inducted into the National Rodeo Hall of Fame, and in 1989 he was inducted into the Pro Rodeo Hall of Fame and the Museum of the American Cowboy. In 1994 he was honored with a U.S. postage stamp, unfortunately the original stamp issued in 1993 featured a photograph of his brother Ben. The mistake was ultimately rectified in 1994 with the release of a stamp based on the marketing poster for the movie *The Bull-Dogger*.

**Crawford Goldsby**

## Crawford Goldsby (Cherokee Bill)
## February 8th, 1876 – March 17, 1896

*"I came here to die, not to make a speech."*
– Crawford Goldsby

Goldsby was a notorious outlaw responsible for the murder of eight people. He was born in Fort Concho, Texas. His father, a mulatto, was a Buffalo Soldier and Sergeant in the Tenth U. S. Cavalry and his mother was part African American, part Cherokee, and part white. Crawford's father George was an interesting fellow who seemed to be constantly on the run either from Southern sympathizers that wanted to lynch him for fighting in the Union Army during the Civil War, or from a deadly racial incident at the Morris Saloon. It seems a group of cowboys and hunters decided they didn't like the idea of black soldiers so they attacked a black sergeant and ripped the chevrons off his sleeve and the stripes from his pants. The sergeant returned to his post gathered a number of black soldiers that returned to the saloon seeking revenge. A gunfight ensued ending with a hunter and a private being killed and several other participants wounded. The Texas Rangers went to the post looking to arrest Goldsby for arming the soldiers that attacked the saloon. Goldsby knew the army wouldn't back him so he escaped into Indian Territory. As a result of his father's absence Crawford bounced around from one family member to another until at age eighteen he began to spiral out of control.

Goldsby got into an argument with Jake Lewis over a disagreement Lewis had with one of Goldsby's brothers. A few days later Goldsby shoots Lewis. Assuming Lewis was dead, Goldsby heads for the Creek and Seminole Nations where he meets Jim and Bill Cook who were part Cherokee. In 1894 the U. S. government purchased a parcel of land from the Cherokee Nation promising to pay two hundred and sixty-five dollars and seventy cents to eligible claimants. Since Goldsby and the Cook brothers were all part Cherokee they figured they were entitled to the payout. Together they made their way to Tahlequah,

Oklahoma, the capital of the Cherokee Nation in order to collect their money.

Since Goldsby was wanted for the Lewis shooting and Jim Cook was wanted for other crimes, they needed to avoid the authorities. They had to find someone who could collect the money for them. They convinced Effie Crittenden who ran a hotel and restaurant to try to get the funds. On her return to the hotel Effie was followed by Sheriff Ellis Rattling Gourd who was hoping to capture Goldsby and Cook. Gourd put together a posse to go after the two outlaws. A gunfight ensued with Deputy Sequoyah Houston killed and Jim Cook wounded. Later on when Sheriff Gourd asked Effie Crittenden if Goldsby was involved in the shootout, she stated that it was the Cooks and *Cherokee Bill*. After their escape, the three men formed the Cook Gang that began robbing banks, stagecoaches, and stores, killing anyone that got in their way.

The last straw came when Goldsby, now known as Cherokee Bill, shot and killed Ernest Melton, who just happened to enter the Shufeldt and Son General Store while it was being robbed. Goldsby was now a marked man with a thirteen hundred dollar reward offered for his capture. Eventually he was caught and taken to Fort Smith, Arkansas where he was tried, convicted, and sentenced to hang for the murder of Ernest Melton.

On July 26. 1895 Sherman Vann, a jail trusty, snuck a Colt revolver into the jail for Goldsby. During the escape attempt, Goldsby shot guard Lawrence Keating in the stomach. When Keating tried to get away, Goldsby shot him again in the back. The attempted escape failed and Goldsby was recaptured. A second trial was held and Goldsby was again convicted and sentenced to hang by notorious hanging judge, Isaac C. Parker. After a series of appeals Goldsby was hanged on March 17th, 1896. When asked if he had any last words, he replied, *"I came here to die, not to make a speech."*

**Nat Love**

## Nat Love (Deadwood Dick)
### June 1854 – 1921

Much of what is known of Nat Love's life as a cowboy comes from his autobiography with the rather long title, *The Life and Adventures of Nat Love, Better Known in the Cattle Country as 'Deadwood Dick.'*

The legend of Nat Love like that of many of the characters of the era is a combination of fact and fiction, of hyperbole and self-promotion blended together and enhanced by a striking photograph of a rugged black-man confidently standing with one hand tucked into his bulleted belt, while the other holds a Winchester Rifle as if it were a gentlemen's walking stick. He wears the obligatory wide-brimmed Stetson pushed back on his head revealing a thick mane of shaggy hair. He stands with one foot posed on his saddle so that all can see he's wearing leather riding chaps. The image is the classic iconic representation of a cowboy.

Nat Love was born a slave on the Robert Love plantation in Davidson County, Tennessee in 1854. His father was the foreman on the plantation and his mother managed the kitchen in the 'big house.' Love's father, Sampson, taught Nat how to read and write despite a law forbidding literacy education for slaves. After the Civil War Nat's family became sharecroppers renting land from their previous owners. Unfortunately Nat's father passed away shortly after harvesting their first crop. Nat had a knack for breaking horses, a skill that would serve him well in the future. The life of a cowboy beckoned.

After winning a horse in a raffle he decided to sell it back to the owner for fifty dollars that he used to leave town. He headed west to Dodge City, Kansas. There he caught on as a cowboy with the Duval Ranch from Texas that had just brought a herd of cattle up to Kansas for shipment back East. In order to win his thirty-dollar a month employment he had to prove himself by breaking a wild horse named *Good Eye*, which he did, claiming later it was the most difficult horse he ever broke. During his time with the

Duval outfit he fought rustlers and Indians, a common occurrence during the post-Civil War period. He became an expert in everything from bronco busting to roping to sharp shooting, earning him his first nickname *Red River Dick*.

In 1872 he moved to Arizona where he got work with the Gallinger Ranch. While there he claimed he met Pat Garrett, Bat Masterson, and Billy The Kid. On July 3rd, 1872 Love arrived in Deadwood, Dakota Territory along with a herd of three thousand cattle. The town was preparing to celebrate the Fourth of July holiday by having a rodeo with a two hundred dollar prize for the all-around cowboy. Love won every contest he entered earning the two hundred dollars as well as his second nickname, *Deadwood Dick*, a reference to a character in Edward Lytton Wheeler's dime novels.

In 1877, while rounding up stray cattle, Love was captured by the Pima Indians. He was shot but not killed. Many of the Pima were of mixed race so they decided to nurse him back to health and adopt him into the tribe; but that didn't appeal to the educated cowboy. He eventually stole a pony and escaped to Texas. Love claims to have been shot fourteen times during his career as a cowboy. In 1889 he decided it was time to quit the frontier life. He married and settled down in Denver taking a job as a Pullman porter overseeing the sleeping cars on the Denver and Rio Grande Railroad. Eventually he moved to Los Angeles, California where he got a job as a courier and guard for the General Securities Company. He died in 1921 at the age of sixty-seven.

**Belle Starr**

# PART III

# THE COWGIRLS

## Belle Starr

### February 5th, 1848 – February 3rd, 1889

*"I regard myself as a woman who has seen much of life."*
- Belle Shirley Reed Starr

Myra Maybelle Shirley Reed Starr was a minor figure in the old west. She became a legend based on the fact that she was a well-educated rich kid from Carthage Missouri who helped run the criminal operations of her various outlaw husbands. She associated with outlaws Jesse James and Cole Younger, was arrested by legendary black lawman Bass Reeves, and tried by Hanging Judge Isaac Parker. She was a woman with style who planned, organized, and participated in stagecoach robberies while riding sidesaddle, wearing her six-shooter around the hips of her signature black velvet riding dress, topped off with a large plumed hat. She was brutally murdered on her way home by an unknown assassin. Belle Starr, *the Bandit Queen*, became the symbolic female outlaw of the Old West.

Belle's father, John Shirley, was the son of a wealthy Virginian family. Her mother was Shirley's third wife. The family settled in Carthage, Missouri where her father made a handsome living from various business enterprises including an inn, livery stable, and blacksmith shop. John Shirley was a respected member of the community. Belle had a proper young ladies education, learning classical languages, and how to play the piano. Despite her society standing there were signs of her wild side. She was taught to ride and shoot by her brother, and somewhere along the line she befriended future outlaws Jesse James and Cole Younger.

Being originally from Virginia, Shirley was a confirmed Confederate supporter. His son Bud became a Captain in Quantrill's Raiders. Missouri was officially a Union state, but it never entered the Civil War due to its pro-slavery population. Neighboring Kansas was a pro-Union state.

After a bloody Union attack on Carthage and the death of his son, Shirley sold his businesses and moved his family to a farm in Scyene, Texas.

**Life of Crime**

In 1866, Jesse James, his brother Frank, and the Youngers robbed a bank in Liberty Missouri stealing six thousand dollars. The Youngers made their way down to Scyene were they hooked up with the Shirleys. Belle is rumored to have been involved with one of the Youngers but no supporting evidence exists to confirm it. What is known is she developed an attachment to another ex-Missourian, Jim Reed, whom she married. In 1868 she gave birth to her daughter Rosie Lee whom she called Pearl. Reed was wanted for murder in Arkansas so the family moved to California for a short while where Belle gave birth to her son, James Edwin Reed. After moving back to Texas, Reed tried farming, but he found the outlaw life more to his liking.

He became involved in the criminal activities of the James-Younger Gang as well as the Cherokee Starr Gang that operated out of the Indian Territory (Oklahoma). In 1869 Belle, Reed, and two others, beat and tortured an Old Creek Indian until he gave up the location where he was hiding thirty thousand dollars in gold. Belle was fast becoming the Bandit Queen of the Old West. In 1874, Reed was killed in Paris, Texas, in a gunfight with another outlaw. After the death of her husband Belle is rumored to have had an affair with one of the Youngers, but there doesn't seem to be any evidence to support the claim. In 1880 Belle married Cherokee outlaw leader Sam Starr. They lived and worked out of the Indian Territory. Belle became integral to the planning and organizing of the gangs cattle rustling, horse stealing, and bootlegging activities. She was also a willing and effective participant in these crimes. Sam and Belle became very successful criminals. They earned enough money to bribe officials if any of their gang members got caught. If bribes weren't the answer to freeing her cohorts, Belle used her female charms to win their freedom.

Fort Smith, Arkansas was the closest settlement to the Starr Gang's operation and the local magistrate Hanging Judge Isaac Parker was determined to see Belle and her husband behind bars. Belle was arrested several times but none of the charges ever stuck until famous black lawman Bass Reeves finally brought her in after she was caught in the act of stealing a neighbor's horse. Both Belle and Sam were convicted. Belle served nine months in the Detroit House of Corrections, in Detroit, Michigan. In 1866 Sam Starr and Officer Frank West killed each other in a gunfight.

## The Unsolved Murder of Belle Starr

The legend of Belle Starr might have faded quickly if not for her mysterious unsolved murder retold and exaggerated in numerous dime novels and tabloid papers. There are several versions of her ambush and murder but none have been verified, and the killer was never found. Like all murder cases, it remains open to this day.

In 1889 two days before her forty-first birthday Belle was ambushed while on the way home from a neighbor's house in Eufaula, Oklahoma. According to this version she was hit with an initial shotgun blast that knocked her off her horse. The murderer then walked up to her while she lay on the ground and shot her again making sure she was dead. Her body was riddled with buckshot wounds to her back, neck, shoulders, and face.

According to *Pistol Pete* Frank Eaton, Belle was on her way home from a dance. Eaton claims he was dancing with Belle when a drunken Edgar Watson tried to cut-in, but Belle declined to dance with him. Watson followed Belle home and while she stopped to water her horse, he shot and killed her. Eaton claims Watson was arrested, tried, convicted, and hanged for the murder but that claim is false as it is known Watson was killed in 1910.

In fact, there appears to be no witnesses to the crime, and no one was ever convicted of the murder despite the fact there were plenty of people with motives. Edgar Watson was a viable suspect based on the premise that he was afraid that Belle would turn him in to the authorities for a murder he committed in Florida. The question is why would she? Her son Ed was suspected of the murder because Belle supposedly beat him for mistreating her horse. Belle's daughter Pearl was also accused of the murder because Belle allegedly interfered in Pearl's marriage. And Belle's current husband a Cherokee named Jim July was also a suspect based on the story that Belle caught him cheating with another woman, causing a lot of trouble in the marriage. The truth will never be known, as to who killed Bell Starr, The Bandit Queen.

Calamity Jane

## Martha Jane Cannary (Calamity Jane)

### May 1st, 1852 – August 1st, 1903

*"I figured, if a girl wants to be a legend, she should just go ahead and be one."*

- Calamity Jane Cannary

Calamity Jane was born in Princeton, Missouri. Her father had a gambling problem and her mother spent time as a prostitute. In 1885 the family moved to Virginia City, Montana. Jane's mother Charlotte died of pneumonia on route. During the long five-month trek, Jane spent time hunting with the men. By the time she reached Virginia City, she was an excellent rider and a crack shot with a rifle. From there her father moved the family to Salt Lake City, Utah where he started a farm, but in 1867 he died. Jane took charge of her five younger siblings moving them first by wagon to Fort Bridger in the Wyoming Territory and then on to Piedmont by railroad. In Piedmont she provided for the family as a dishwasher, cook, waitress, dance-hall girl, nurse, ox team driver, and sometime prostitute at the Fort Laramie Three-Mile Hog Ranch. Prostitution was a familiar occupation for women without other means of support. In 1874 Jane found work as a scout in Fort Russell.

## Calamity Jane, Heroine of the Plains

Jane was illiterate, itinerant, and an alcoholic, but by her own account she was brave to the point of reckless. She claims she received the *Calamity* moniker from a Captain Egan while working as a scout out of Goose Greek, Wyoming in 1872 or '73. Jane was scouting for Captain Egan when they were order to put down an Indian uprising. During the mission the troop was attacked a number of times with six soldiers killed and several others wounded. On the way back to the Post, Jane was riding on ahead when the soldiers were attacked again. On hearing the gunfire she turned to see Captain Egan shot. Jane quickly turned and rode back to Egan grabbing him just before he was about to fall. Jane managed to get Egan onto her horse and get him safely back to the Fort. While recovering Captain Egan is supposed to have said, *"I name you Calamity, the heroine of the plains."*

There are those that dispute her account and she was known to exaggerate her claims. Another version of how the nickname came about was that those who dared offend her *"courted calamity."* However she acquired the name, it was well established by 1876 when she arrived in Deadwood, Dakota Territory with the Charlie Utter and Wild Bill Hickok wagon train. On July 15th, 1876, The Black Hills Pioneer announced, *"Calamity Jane has arrived."* She settled in Deadwood and despite the toll her rugged lifestyle had on her appearance, she was sporadically employed by Dora DuFran, a local madam.

Jane made other claims some of which could be true like giving birth to two daughters; others were more likely false, like the claim she married Hickok and that one of her daughters was his. She also claimed she went after Hickok's killer with a meat cleaver which again is probably a figment of her drunken imagination. Evidently she did save a stagecoach from being attacked on its way to Deadwood. When the driver, John Slaughter, was killed during the ambush, Jane was able to take control and get the stagecoach to its destination. Jane did have a compassionate side, helping nurse smallpox victims during an epidemic that broke out in Deadwood sometime in 1876 or 1878.

In 1881 Jane moved on to Miles City, Montana and bought a ranch and opened an inn. She married Texan Clinton Burke, moved to Boulder, and gave birth to a daughter that she gave up for adoption. In 1883 she started appearing in

Buffalo Bill's Wild West show spinning tall tales of her frontier exploits. In 1903, she managed to get back to a small mining village near Deadwood where she died due to pneumonia and inflammation of the bowels. Martha Jane Cannary is buried at the Mount Moriah Cemetery, South Dakota, next to her friend Wild Bill Hickok.

Ellen Liddy Watson

## Ellen Liddy Watson (Cattle Kate)
## July 2nd, 1860 – July 20th, 1889

*"Witnesses were murdered... disappeared mysteriously or were bought off. The three Cheyenne papers, dominated by incredibly wealthy cattle interests, trumped-up the ridiculous stories... about Ellen being a dirty whore and rustler, and Jim her accomplice, pimp and murderous paramour."*
- George W. Hufsmith
*The Wyoming Lynching of Cattle Kate, 1889*

Ellen (Ella) Watson and her husband Jim Averell were lynched for defying the large cattle baron interests of the Wyoming Stock Growers Association. After murdering Watson and Averell the WSGA used their strong-arm muscle to scare off or eliminate witnesses; they then used their political and media influence to destroy the reputations of their victims and justify their crimes. There is a theme that runs through the stories of the Old West: failure to understand the historical significance of injustice condemns society to repeat those mistakes and the consequences associated with them. Society ultimately pays the price when money, muscle, and media influence are used by big business to destroy the reputation and lives of those that stand in the way of their pursuit of economic dominance.

Ella Watson was born in Bruce County, Ontario to Scottish parents, Thomas Lewis Watson and Francis Close. Ellen was the oldest of ten children. The family moved to Kansas where Ella had the misfortune to marry William Pickell an abusive drunk. She left Pickell and eventually divorced him, ultimately heading out to Denver, Colorado to join one of her brothers. She bounced around the South West working as a cook, waitress, and seamstress until she got a job in Sweetwater River, Wyoming working for Jim Averell who operated a restaurant and general store.

Watson and Averell married but kept it quiet in order for both to qualify for land under the Homestead Act of 1862. The legislation allowed single, but not married women to buy one hundred and sixty acres of land provided they improved the property within five years. Watson and Averell owned adjacent properties. Watson had a small cabin, and a corral built on her property in order to meet the Homestead Act requirement. She earned extra money by doing seamstress work for local cowboys. The constant visits to her cabin by men led to the false rumors that she was a prostitute. With her savings she bought a small herd of cattle.

Ella fenced in about sixty acres of her land with barbed wire controlling about one mile of the water along Horse Creek. The severe winter snowfalls made it difficult for cattle to graze, putting a premium on access to the water needed to grow hay to feed the cattle over the winter. The fencing of the waterway cut the amount of water going to the neighboring ranch owned by Albert John Bothwell, a member of the powerful Wyoming Stock Growers Association (WSGA). The Association controlled and policed the cattle industry in Wyoming and they continually put the squeeze on small ranchers like Ella Watson. Bothwell repeatedly attempted to purchase Ella's

WSGA built portable cabins that they moved around the area establishing homesteads, eventually registering ownership of the land around the Watson ranch. The strategy eliminated access to open range grazing for the small ranchers like Ella Watson.

The WSGA made a law that claimed all maverick cattle were automatically owned by the WSGA and were to be branded with the "M" brand. They also established a law that demanded all ranchers have an approved registered brand in order to claim ownership to their cattle. The cost of registering established by the association was exorbitant, but despite the cost, Ella applied five times over three years, but each time her application was denied. She finally purchased the "LU" brand from fellow local rancher John Crowder. In 1888 Ella bought twenty-eight cattle from a herd on its way to the Salt Lake basin from Nebraska. By the next year her herd had grown to forty-one head.

Bothwell and the WSGA upped the harassment of Ella and Jim Averell. George Henderson a so-called range detective that worked for the WSGA noticed the fresh "LU" brand on the new cattle and accused Ella and Jim of rustling. A meeting was held and six members of the association, including Bothwell, decided to take matters into their own hands. The vigilante group tore down the Watson fence driving Ella's cattle off her property. Both Ella and Jim Averell were taken into custody and told they were to be taken to Rawlings.

The abduction was witnessed by Gene Crowder who was living and working on the Watson ranch. Crowder ran to Averell's house where he told Frank Buchanan what had happened. Buchanan went after the posse. He saw from a distance that the posse had stopped and were tying ropes around Jim and Ella's necks. He opened fire, but when the group started firing back, he had to withdraw as he was badly outnumbered. Ella Watson and Jim Averell where left hanging for two and a half days before they were finally cut down.

The six vigilantes led by Bothwell were all arrested but released on five thousand dollar bonds. At this point a series of mysterious disappearances and murders took place. Gene Crowder, Frank Buchanan, and John DeCorey, a boy that worked for Ella, all disappeared. Jim Averell's nephew, Ralph Cole, mysteriously died the very day he was supposed to testify before the Grand Jury. With no one left to testify, all the charges were dropped. There were other witnesses including neighboring small ranchers and even newspaper reporters, but none came forward to testify for fear of reprisal.

The newspapers were in the pocket of the WSGA, leading to a series of articles branding Ella Watson, *Cattle Kate*, a rustler. The incident led to the formation of the Northern Wyoming Farmers and Stock Growers Association, a group in direct competition to the WSGA, leading to the infamous Johnson County War.

## Etta Place

### Birth: Unknown – Death: Unknown

Of the dozens of major and minor outlaws, lawmen, and characters that were researched for this book almost everyone had a birth and death date recorded no matter how minor or insignificant their history. Why is there no record of the birth, death, or family background of Etta Place? The woman who used the name existed, but who was she, where did she come from, and what ultimately happened to her? Etta Place appeared from nowhere to join the Wild Bunch entourage and just as mysteriously disappeared shortly after the presumed deaths of Robert Leroy Parker and Harry Alonzo Longabaugh.

Even her name is a mystery: was she Ethel, Ethal, Eva, Rita, Etta, or none of the aforementioned? And the surname Place was most certainly borrowed. She might have been a schoolteacher or married to a schoolteacher; she might have had two children that she abandoned for Longabaugh; or she might have been a prostitute working at Madame Fannie Porter's San Antonio brothel. She might have been all these people, or she might have been none of them.

Who was Etta Place? Did she actually exist, or was she really Ann Bassett or someone else? People… especially people with a reputation just don't disappear unless it's on purpose. We know she was the girlfriend of the Sundance Kid; we know she was attractive; and we know she disappeared sometime in 1909 when Longabaugh and Parker supposedly died in a murder-suicide in Bolivia.

Did Etta Place disappear with Longabaugh after he returned from Bolivia when two other American outlaws were mistaken for Butch and Sundance? After all… don't all gringos look alike? An exaggerated claim of killing the infamous Butch Cassidy and Sundance Kid would have been a feather in the cap of the Bolivian Army; something dozens of U. S. lawman and the Pinkerton Detective Agency couldn't do.

Perhaps Etta Place doesn't even belong in this book because she wasn't like Laura Bullion, a full-fledged member of the Wild Bunch who joined in the robbing of trains and banks along with the rest of the male members of the gang. On the other hand, Place may have participated in some robberies while in Argentina, and if she was really Ann Bassett as is speculated, then she did provide valuable services to the gang beyond mere female companionship. In any case, Place was one of a handful of women that were allowed into the inner circle of the Wild Bunch, allowed to enter the Hole-In-The-Wall hideout, and the one woman Butch and Sundance took to Bolivia when they fled the U. S. A.

According to various Pinkerton reports and hospital records it is estimated that she was born sometime around 1878. There are two existing photographs of her as well as reports alluding to her good looks, nice personality, and ability with a firearm. In almost all cases the descriptions and images could be substituted for rancher and Wild Bunch intimate Ann Bassett. This speculation takes on even more substance when you take into account that "Place" was most likely not her real name. "Place" was Longabaugh's mother's maiden name (Ann Place). It would be quite a coincidence if Longabaugh met a woman that had the same name as his mother. She was even known at times as Mrs. Harry A. Place. Even her first name morphed over time from Ethel to Eva to Rita, and finally Etta.

Of the two existing images of Place the most famous is the portrait of her and Longabaugh in New York at the DeYoung Portrait Studio. The image was taken just after a visit to Tiffany's where Sundance bought a diamond stickpin for himself and a lapel watch for Etta. The watch can be seen in the photograph.

**So Who Was Etta Place?**
Was Etta Place really Ethel Bishop, originally from West Virginia, an unemployed music teacher that lived around the corner from Fannie Porter's brothel; and who made a few dollars moonlighting at Fannie's establishment where she met Parker and Longabaugh?

Was she really Madaline Wilson, a British-born prostitute that lived and worked in Porter's whorehouse, and who disappeared off the census rolls after 1900, coincidently around the time Place is rumored to have runoff with Longabaugh? This idea has some credibility as Place was always described as having a refined way of speaking, something that could be chalked up to an Americanized British accent. As well, several of the Wild Bunch women worked for Fannie Porter from time to time.

The most compelling choice seems to be Ann Bassett, the rancher, rustler, and Wild Bunch groupie that some, including the Pinkerton Detective Agency, described in almost the exact same manner as Etta Place. Comparisons of existing photographs showed two women that could be dead-ringers for one another. Dr. Thomas G. Kyle of the Computer Research Group at Los Alamos National Laboratory confirmed that the two women were the same person based on his analysis of the photographs.

Historian Doris Karren Burton investigated the two

women. In her book published in 1992, she states the two women were the same. The only fly in the ointment is Ann Bassett was arrested, sent to jail, and married while Etta Place was supposedly in South America, but can anything about these two women be relied on as fact.

There were Pinkerton reports that someone that looked like Etta Place was killed in a domestic dispute while in Argentina. Another report says she committed suicide in Argentina in 1924 while yet another states she died of natural causes In 1966. Some say Etta Place became Edith Mae when she married Tex Rickard, the promoter of the Jack Johnson-Jim Jeffries boxing match, after which the couple retired to a ranch in Paraguay. Each new fact or rumor concerning Etta Place creates more questions than it does answers. She was definitely the most mysterious woman of the Old West. The Etta Place mystery continues.

# Epilogue
## The Myth of The American Psyche

Nations like people have personalities; there is a collective consciousness, an overriding pervasive self-image that countries have of themselves that may differ greatly from how others see them. America may not care what others think but they should. Failure to understand your real self, and how external forces view it, can be dangerous.

Understanding why things are the way they are requires a realistic understanding of history. Not the glamorized Hollywood cardboard cutout version of the nineteen fifties. Not the whitewashed grade school version that glosses over the nasty, lurid parts; but rather the unvarnished truth, with all its warts, scabs, and failures.

The real American cowboy goes to the core of the true collective psyche of the United States, not the false consciousness of the high-minded platitudes engraved on statues.

Look closely at America and you'll see the real Wyatt Earp, the real Bill Hickok, the real cowboys, lawmen, and outlaws that molded the American personality. Understand them, and you'll understand who and what America is.

**Wyatt Earp**
**The Quintessential Cowboy, Lawman, & Outlaw**

# References

- lingerandlook.com/Names/Cowboys3.htm
- en.wikipedia.org/wiki/Bat_Masterson
- en.wikipedia.org/wiki/Quanah_Parker
- apstudynotes.org/us-history/topics/cattle-frontiers-and-farming/
- legendsofamerica.com/we-buffalohunters.html
- owlcation.com/humanities/Black-Outlaws-Cowboys-And-Lawmen-Of-The-Old-West
- en.wikipedia.org/wiki/Wyatt_Earp
- tombstonetimes.com/stories/benson.html
- tombstonetimes.com/stories/wyatt.html
- csgv.org/blog/2011/getting-to-know-doc-holliday/
- en.wikipedia.org/wiki/Johnny_Ringo
- www.johnnyringo.com/jrtexas.html
- en.wikipedia.org/wiki/Doc_Scurlock
- rehtwogunraconteur.com/doc-scurlock-from-lincoln-county-to-eastland-county/
- en.wikipedia.org/wiki/Lawrence_Murphy
- en.wikipedia.org/wiki/Tom_Horn
- historynet.com/tom-horn-misunderstood-misfit.htm

- en.wikipedia.org/wiki/Charles_B._Gatewood
- en.wikipedia.org/wiki/Pleasant_Valley_War
- en.wikipedia.org/wiki/%22Wild_Bill%22_Hickok
- en.wikipedia.org/wiki/Banditti_of_the_Prairie
- en.wikipedia.org/wiki/Utah_War
- en.wikipedia.org/wiki/McCanles_Gang
- en.wikipedia.org/wiki/John_Wesley_Hardin
- frontiertimes.com/outlaws/hardin.html
- history.com/news/history-lists/9-things-you-may-not-know-about-billy-the-kid
- en.wikipedia.org/wiki/Billy_the_Kid
- en.wikipedia.org/wiki/Lincoln_County_Regulators
- legendsofamerica.com/we-bellestarr.html
- en.wikipedia.org/wiki/Belle_Starr
- legendsofamerica.com/ks-bleedingkansas.html
- en.wikipedia.org/wiki/Sundance_Kid
- en.wikipedia.org/wiki/Butch_Cassidy
- en.wikipedia.org/wiki/Jesse_James
- en.wikipedia.org/wiki/Cole_Younger
- legendsofamerica.com/we-youngerbrothers.html
- en.wikipedia.org/wiki/Bleeding_Kansas

- theappendix.net/issues/2014/1/bandit-resurrections-who-was-the-real-sundance-kid
- en.wikipedia.org/wiki/Sundance_Kid
- http://chroniclingamerica.loc.gov
- en.wikipedia.org/wiki/Bass_Reeves
- en.wikipedia.org/wiki/Nat_Love
- en.wikipedia.org/wiki/George_R._Reeves
- listverse.com/2016/04/04/10-african-american-cowboys-who-shaped-the-old-west/
- blackpast.org/aaw/isom-dart-1849-1900
- horsehints.org/CowboysWorld/BlackIsomDart.htm
- en.wikipedia.org/wiki/Tom_Horn
- en.wikipedia.org/wiki/Bill_Pickett
- en.wikipedia.org/wiki/Crawford_Goldsby
- en.wikipedia.org/wiki/Nat_Love
- legendsofamerica.com/we-natlove.html
- history.com/news/history-lists/7-things-you-might-not-know-about-jesse-james
- history.com/news/history-lists/6-things-you-might-not-know-about-butch-cassidy
- en.wikipedia.org/wiki/Butch_Cassidy

- en.wikipedia.org/wiki/Hole-in-the-Wall
- criminalelement.com/blogs/2011/08/the-mysterious-disappearance-of-etta-place
- en.wikipedia.org/wiki/Etta_Place
- en.wikipedia.org/wiki/Big_Nose_Kate
- newsmax.com/FastFeatures/girls-with-guns-quotes-calamity-jane/2015/04/16/id/638993/
- en.wikipedia.org/wiki/Calamity_Jane
- en.wikipedia.org/wiki/Ellen_Watson
- en.wikipedia.org/wiki/Johnson_County_War
- legendsofamerica.com/we-cattlekate.html
- en.wikipedia.org/wiki/Mary_Fields
- badassoftheweek.com/fields.html
- en.wikipedia.org/wiki/Elfego_Baca
- en.wikipedia.org/wiki/Luke_Short
- www.legendsofamerica.com/we-lukeshort.html
- www.artofmanliness.com/2011/04/24/lessons-in-manliness-from-bass-reeves/

# The Outlaw Rider

by Jerry Bader

Illustrated by Paola Ceccantoni

# Organized Crime Queens
## The Secret World of Female Gangsters

Written by Jerry Bader
Illustrated by Dream Computers

www.ingramcontent.com/pod-product-compliance
Lightning Source LLC
Chambersburg PA
CBHW070055080526
44586CB00013B/1060